Ri

King David
and
Other Kings

Life Lessons for Today

King David and Other Kings: Life Lessons for Today

ISBN: 978-1-64370-623-8

Published by:
Rich Kanyali Ministries
P.O Box 243
Woodland Park CO 80866

RichKanyaliministries.com

info@richkanyaliministries.com

Acknowledgments and Special Thanks.

I would like also to give special thanks to the following people who have made and continue to make a major positive impact on my life:

Andrew Wommack - It's an absolute privilege to serve at your ministry. I have learned a lot from you over the past many years. You have taught and inspired me so much. Your humility is very admirable. Your teachings helped in quickening me to write this book. Thank you, so very much.

Pastor Greg Mohr (Director of Charis Bible College). Pastor Greg, you are a man of wisdom and humility. You have taught me so much. Thank you for pouring out your heart to help grow, change, and impact my life. I'm forever grateful.

Pastor Rick McFarland (Dean of Education, Charis Bible College). Pastor Rick, you are my Pastor and mentor. I look up to you and I greatly appreciate all you have invested in me and spoken in my life. Thank you very much.

Thank you all for impacting and changing my life.

Table of Contents

Other Kings (King Jehu, Manasseh, Josiah, Saul, and Jehoshaphat)

Introduction

In this book, I take a journey into the lives of Kings David, Jehu, Saul, Jehoshaphat, Manasseh, and Josiah. There are tremendous things we can learn from the lives of those who have gone before us; in studying them, we not only learn the good in their lives, but we also learn the bad and how to avoid it. We can learn what to do and what NOT to do.

King David is one of the kings in the Bible who has a very detailed life. The Bible hides nothing about him. It clearly shows his good and his ugly, his childhood through his growth: from a shepherd boy, to a king over Judah, and, finally, King over Israel.

There is a great deal to consider and take away from the lives of these men that I strongly believe will impact your life for the better.

Personally, as I started to study all the kings of Israel, I found a wealth of practical things that can be applied to our lives today and this prompted me to write and compile this book.

My sincere prayer is that you will take at least a single truth and let it revolutionize your entire life.

I also want to say that I have personally never read a book (besides the Holy Bible) where I pretty much agreed with everything the author said however; I learn hundreds of things and I will not let one thing I disagree with hinder me from learning the rest of the things written.

In saying that, feel free to disagree where you want to disagree. I have personally written this book and I have complete belief and confidence in everything I've written. This book has impacted my life and I hope it does the same for you.

King David

Accepting Responsibility

It all started in the Garden where, when man sinned, he did not take responsibility for his actions, but passed the buck to the woman and then to God. He said "The woman whom thou gavest to be with me, she gave me of the tree, and I did eat" (Genesis 3:12). Notice that he said "the woman whom thou gavest to be with me."

The woman never forced the man to eat. She did not shove the "apple" down his throat, but the man who willfully took the fruit and ate it, and then he refused to take responsibility and blamed the woman and God.

Naturally, no one wants to take responsibility for what they have done wrong. Man will find some way to blame someone else for his mistakes. I believe this is a result of the sin nature that we inherited from Adam when he sinned. Look no further; the world we live in is full of this, and this is one of the reasons we have so many issues in our societies. Everyone says, "It's not my fault. It's your fault. It is my father's fault that my life turned out this way, and, by the way, I just turned forty years old."

What? At such an age people are still blaming others for what happened thirty years ago. We all have had some sort of dysfunction in our families; some indeed more than others. There is no perfect family, but many choose to blame another person besides themselves for how things have turned out.

True, there might have been something wrong done to you, but are you going to live the rest of your life pointing your finger, or are you going to rise up and begin to change the course of your life? I'm not saying that you take responsibility for what others have done, but I'm saying that you begin to make decisions and take responsibility for what you have not done that you should have done.

I have a black skin color by description (I'm not black, black is not who I am), but I never ever see things in light of the color of my skin. I don't hide behind it. I have risen up and seen things in light of God's Word, and I have been able to take my life to another level. I refuse to believe, or even consider, that the reason I should never rise up is because of the color of my skin. I take responsibility and refuse to blame the color of my skin as the reason for my failures or lack of success thereof. Now, I do know that there are still some issues in regard to color in the world, but that will not hold me back. I am a child of God and that supersedes the color of my skin. I do not see myself as black. I see myself as a child of God who has enormous favor, wisdom, and power. I have the same enabling and ability as anyone else. I am a child of the Most High God.

"Yeah, right, I don't agree with you," you may be thinking. Well, neither do I agree with you. If I were to agree with you, we would both be wrong. And by the way, don't wake me up, because it has been working for me pretty well.

In stark contrast to King Saul, David was a man who took responsibility and admitted to his wrongdoing every time he sinned. He repented and asked for forgiveness and blamed no one else—not God and not the people.

In 2 Samuel 11, we see how David steals another man's wife and commits adultery with her. In an effort to cover up his gross sin, he plans, and succeeds, in murdering the husband of the woman. When David was confronted by the Prophet Nathan in 2 Samuel 12, David repented and took responsibility for his wrong actions. David did not blame the men he sent to fetch Bathsheba, nor did he blame anyone else. He took full responsibility.

> *And David spoke unto the LORD when he saw the angel that smote the people, and said, Lo, I have sinned, and I have done wickedly: but these sheep, what have they done? let thine hand, I pray thee, be against me, and against my father's house.*
>
> — 2 Samuel 24:17

In 2 Samuel 24, we see another sin from David where he counted the people against God's command. When he was confronted by the Prophet Gad for his sin, again, David did not look around and blame someone else. He took full responsibility for his sin.

Although the consequences were very severe, he never tried to excuse himself, shift blame, or try to place it on other people. David made some grave mistakes, and even though the Bible calls him a man after God's own heart, it was not because he was sinless. It was because his response was a heart turned toward God whenever he blew it. What a great character!

Today, some of us are taught to blame someone else for all of our mess. We are taught that it's not our fault even if it's us who have sinned. We take no responsibility for our actions and behavior.

As long as we play victims, we will never experience the true victory God has for us. This victim mentality and attitude is destroying countless lives today.

I will go into detail later on responsibility because this is one of the main highlights of David's life.

Chosen By God

And the LORD said unto Samuel, How long wilt thou mourn for Saul, seeing I have rejected him from reigning over Israel? Fill thine horn with oil, and go, I will send thee to Jesse the Bethlehemite: for I have provided me a king among his sons.

— 1 Samuel 16:1

David was chosen; he did not promote himself to be king. The Lord sought out David and called him to this position of king over Israel.

We should never promote ourselves or call ourselves into ministry. We must be called and chosen by God. We must do only that which God has called us to do. We also see that after David was called, he was anointed for the office or ministry God had called and chosen for him to do. Today, many people follow the wishes of their parents and go into the ministry. Others go in because everyone in their family was a minister.

God is not calling people into ministry because of their family tree or heritage. Seek God for yourself and hear from Him personally. Has God called you or are you calling your self? If you are going to last in ministry, you want to make sure God has called and chosen you. David was chosen by God, not man.

And call Jesse to the sacrifice, and I will show thee what thou shalt do: and thou shalt anoint unto me him whom I name unto thee.

— 1 Samuel 16:3

God Looks On The Heart

But the LORD said unto Samuel, Look not on his countenance, or on the height of his stature; because I have refused him: for the LORD seeth not as man seeth; for man looketh on the outward appearance, but the LORD looketh on the heart.

— 1 Samuel 16:7

Most people are impressed and make decisions based on carnal things such as height, looks, eloquence, education, popularity, fame, wealth, money, status, color, and so forth. But not God.

But God hath chosen the foolish things of the world to confound the wise; and God hath chosen the weak things of the world to confound the things which are mighty; And base things of the world, and things which are despised, hath God chosen, yea, and things which are not, to bring to naught things that are: That no flesh should glory in his presence.

— 1 Corinthians 1:27-29

Samuel was no different in this particular case. He was focused on the outside appearance of Eliab and thought, "Here was the Lord's anointed." I believe this was influenced by his experience when he was anointing King Saul. 1 Samuel 9:2 says, "And he had a son, whose name was Saul, a choice young man, and a goodly: and there was not among the children of Israel a goodlier person than he: from his shoulders and upward he was higher than any of the people."

Samuel thought that God was going to choose someone in the lines of physical stature and so forth; however, the Lord told Samuel that Eliab was not the chosen one. We have to learn this principle and lesson. Samuel, a godly prophet, almost missed God because of his focus on the physical.

God chooses the very things that are despised and overlooked (David), despised of men (David) to confound the wise (Samuel and Jesse).

Never Forgotten

And Samuel said unto Jesse, Are here all thy children? And he said, There remaineth yet the youngest, and, behold, he keepeth the sheep. And Samuel said unto Jesse, Send and fetch him: for we will not sit down till he come hither. And he sent, and brought him in. Now he was ruddy, and withal of a beautiful countenance, and goodly to look to. And the LORD said, Arise, anoint him: for this is he.

— 1 Samuel 16:11-12

Sometimes, we go through life or certain situations thinking no one sees and no one cares. Have you ever been down that road? Here is the good news: just like in the situation with David, God never forgets you. God is always mindful of us. He is always thinking of us. He will not forget us even if it looks like men have.

We must continue to be faithful even when it looks like it is useless. Be faithful in the little (Luke 16:10), and do all unto the Lord not unto men (Colossians 3:17, 22-24). It seems like no one was watching David in the bush keeping sheep, but God was (2 Chronicles 16:9). The forgotten one ended up being remembered and elevated above all those who were not forgotten. The last became the first. Thank You, Jesus!

Faithful In The Little

And Samuel said unto Jesse, Are here all thy children? And he said, There remaineth yet the youngest, and, behold, <u>he keepeth the sheep</u>. And Samuel said unto Jesse, Send and fetch him: for we will not sit down till he come hither.

— 1 Samuel 16:11 (underline mine)

David started out as a sheep keeper. He did not start on top. Most people do not want to start from the bottom and rise through the ranks. They want to be hired today and get promoted tomorrow. They want to be paid as one who has been with the company for years. Most people are not realistic at all. But life teaches this lesson, and we learn from

David's life, that we must first be faithful in the very little and God will promote us to the bigger (Psalms 75:6). It is a process. First the blade, then the ear, then the full corn in the ear (Mark 4:28). No one climbs a ladder from the top!

As David was being faithful in the least, God was creating in him the heart of a leader. He was preparing him for the throne, although David may not have known that. God does not prepare us at the top for the top, but prepares us for the top at the bottom. If we cannot be faithful in the very little, we will not be faithful in much. We must do things with excellence and faithfulness however small they are.

While David was in the bush keeping sheep, he grew in his relationship with God, and also came to the knowledge of God's covenant with the nation of Israel. He was faithful in the bush (secret), but was promoted before every eye (public). God surely sees in secret. Be faithful in the little. One may say, "I have been faithful in this and that, but I have waited and waited and I have not seen anything come through for me." If you cannot be promoted where you are, God will have someone take you away and promote you. God will promote you somewhere else. Do not kick down doors. Do not promote yourself.

The Holy Spirit Upon Him

Then Samuel took the horn of oil, and anointed him in the midst of his brethren: and the Spirit of the LORD came upon David from that day forward. So Samuel rose up, and went to Ramah.

— 1 Samuel 16:13

I know that all born-again believers have the Spirit of God, but when one is filled with the Holy Spirit, they not only HAVE the Holy Spirit, but the Holy Spirit HAS them. He is not just in them, but now He is on them, flowing out of them and influencing their lives BIG TIME. The Holy Spirit baptism is very crucial in our lives.

The Spirit of God came upon David after he was anointed king over Israel. I believe one of the reasons for this was that David could not do the job of a king without supernatural empowerment and ability. He could not do it in his own strength.

This same thing happened to King Saul when he was anointed king (1 Samuel 10:6). In the same way, a Christian will struggle to live a victorious Christian life in his own strength. It is actually impossible to live and do exploits for the kingdom of God without being endued with power (Acts 1:8). We need the power of the Holy Spirit of whom many of us are missing out.

The Lord Is With Us

Then answered one of the servants, and said, Behold, I have seen a son of Jesse the Bethlehemite, that is cunning in playing, and a mighty valiant man, and a man of war, and prudent in matters, and a comely person, and the LORD is with him.

— 1 Samuel 16:18

Notice that David was given a job before he applied to play the harp for the king. The servant of the king knew a lot about David. How did he know all these things about David that were cultivated in the bush? He said David was good at playing, a mighty valiant man, a man of war, prudent in matters, a comely person, and the Lord was with him. There had to be something noticeable about David for this servant to say that God was with him.

I happen to believe it was David's heart and attitude that made a major difference. It was contagious. David never kicked down this door, even if he had a very impressive resume. He got a recommendation from the king's servant.

We must remember that David was a young boy at this time, and being called a man of war and a mighty valiant man has to be a reference to David killing the lion and the bear (1 Samuel 17:34-35). I think the most striking and impressing thing about David's resume was that the Lord was with him. Everything else would have been useless had the Lord not been with him. That made the biggest difference.

The Lord used probably the least impressive thing on David's resume to get him before the king — that he was a master musician. The Lord is with you. This is the most important part of your resume. At least it was for David, and look how far he went. Hallelujah!

Favor

And David came to Saul, and stood before him: and he loved him greatly; and he became his armor bearer. And Saul sent to Jesse, saying, Let David, I pray thee, stand before me; for he hath found favor in my sight.

— 1 Samuel 16:21-22

David was loved by Saul as soon as he stood before him. There is no better way to explain why than to look at what the scripture says. It says that it's all because he found favor in King Saul's sight. It had to be God who got David there, because from a natural standpoint, this was dangerous to David's life. David looked good only because of God's favor and anointing on his life.

If a man under the Old Testament, which was an inferior testament, had favor with man and with God, how much more do we have favor, who are under the new superior testament of grace?

But now hath he obtained a more excellent ministry, by how much also he is the mediator of a better covenant, which was established upon better promises.

— Hebrews 8:6

Persistent Faithfulness

But David went and returned from Saul to feed his father's sheep at Bethlehem.

— 1 Samuel 17:15

Even if David had a "new job" with King Saul as a musician, he never neglected his responsibility of keeping his father's sheep. He was a hardworking man. He continued to feed his father's sheep. We see that even when he was sent by his father to take his brother's food, David was responsible enough to have a keeper take care of the sheep in his absence.

We should not neglect our primary responsibilities until we assign them to another or raise up another to take our place. David also remained subject to his father even though he knew very well he was anointed to be king.

Evoke The Covenant

And the men of Israel said, Have ye seen this man that is come up? surely to defy Israel is he come up: and it shall be, that the man who killeth him, the king will enrich him with great riches, and will give him his daughter, and make his father's house free in Israel. And David spoke to the men that stood by him, saying, What shall be done to the man that killeth this Philistine, and taketh away the reproach from Israel? for who is this uncircumcised Philistine, that he should defy the armies of the living God?
— 1 Samuel 17:25-26

David had a relationship with the Lord. He knew that God had a covenant with the children of Israel, but not with the Philistines. He knew that by calling upon the promises in God's covenant, Goliath was up against God, not Israel or David.

David knew that he was the one with a covenant with God and that is why he called Goliath an "uncircumcised Philistine." We also, as children of God, have a covenant with God, and we should refuse to settle for anything but victory. Our enemies are in trouble because we are children of the covenant. David was not looking at his physical abilities to take down this giant. He was looking at the spiritual, specifically God's promises to His children with a covenant.

We must study God's Word, learn of the promises He has for us, and use these promises to stand against our enemies (Psalms 107:20 and Isaiah 54:17).

Prepare Your Heart To Seek The Lord

And David rose up early in the morning, and left the sheep with a keeper, and took, and went, as Jesse had commanded him; and he came to the trench, as the host was going forth to the fight, and shouted for the battle.

— 1 Samuel 17:20

David shouted for the battle, which implies he was neither afraid nor scared. He was excited to see the demise of the Philistines. We should have the same attitude and go hard after any "Goliath" with a shout of victory and cheer, knowing we are going to conquer. Even when the enemy intimidated and spoke negative words against the children of Israel, David was strong and not afraid.

His reaction was predetermined long before he came to experience the challenge of Goliath because he had prepared his heart to seek the Lord while he was still in the bush keeping sheep. This is the reason David did not flee into hiding when the rest of the Israelites were fleeing. He was not paralyzed by the threat of Goliath. His heart was prepared (2 Chronicles 12:14) and fixed ahead of time, before this crisis came.

What we do when there is no pressure or no crisis determines what we will do when pressure and crisis hits.

Preparation of our hearts to seek the Lord, to live a godly life, and to overcome temptation is not accidental. It doesn't just happen. We prepare in all areas of life such as business, careers, battle and so forth, but not this area. Why is it? You will not live godly or overcome the temptation and evil of this life accidentally. There has to be effort and work on your part. Confidence is preparation. Our confidence comes from our preparation.

"By failing to prepare, you are preparing to fail."
—Benjamin Franklin

"Prepare the umbrella before it rains." —Malay Proverb

"The best preparation for tomorrow is doing your best today."
—H. Jackson Brown Jr.

Keep Your Eyes On The Fruit

And the men of Israel said, Have ye seen this man that is come up? surely to defy Israel is he come up: and it shall be, that the man who killeth him, the king will enrich him with great riches, and will give him his daughter, and make his father's house free in Israel.

— 1 Samuel 17:25

There was a reward to be given to the man who would destroy Goliath, but all the soldiers of Israel were in hiding. They could not look beyond the problem (the giant) to the reward. It was quite a big reward: a wife, great riches, and his father's house would be made free.

We all face challenges in life, but we must keep our eyes on the fruit. We cannot endure or take on challenges if we do not keep our eyes on the fruit. Jesus was able to endure the cross because He looked at and focused on the fruit (Hebrews 12:2-3).

Our eyes should be fixed on the prize, not the challenge or the problem (Philippians 3:13-14). Just like a runner who is focused on the reward, he can endure pretty much anything to get to that reward or prize. A reward is a good motivation to keep us on track.

We must keep our eyes on the fruit and not get weary or intimidated. David kept his eyes on the fruit. He was never discouraged and he got the fruit (reward).

Criticism Will Come

And Eliab his eldest brother heard when he spoke unto the men; and Eliab's anger was kindled against David, and he said, Why camest thou down hither? and with whom hast thou left those few sheep in the wilderness? I know thy pride, and the naughtiness of thine heart; for thou art come down that thou mightest see the battle.

— 1 Samuel 17:28

And Saul said to David, Thou art not able to go against this Philistine to fight with him: for thou art but a youth, and he a man of war from his youth.

— 1 Samuel 17:33

Whenever you choose to embark on a godly journey or a God-given assignment, you will be criticized because many people cannot make your level. For some people, because they cannot make your level and standard you have set for yourself, the best they can do is bring you down to theirs through slander and criticism. This ploy makes them feel good about themselves.

David, being the man of faith he was, did not escape criticism. He got criticized by Eliab for thinking out-of-the-box. Eliab was jealous of David because he was anointed king. Eliab had no valid reason to criticize David. David was responsible; he had left the sheep with a keeper. Additionally, David did not come to the battle on his own; he was sent by his father. Eliab was angry, but the bottom line was he was jealous. He was unhappy that God had passed him by to choose David. He was trying to get back at David in this situation.

There was no wickedness in David's heart as Eliab had said. This was a man after God's heart. Eliab was just a jealous and angry guy.

Criticism did not stop with Eliab. King Saul also had some criticism to bring to David.

And Saul said to David, Thou art not able to go against this Philistine to fight with him: for thou art but a youth, and he a man of war from his youth.

— 1 Samuel 17:33

King Saul called him a youth. David was a youth, but a very experienced youth, and the chosen king-to-be who also had the anointing of God on his life. David was not an average youth; he was also a man of war. He had seen, and defeated, stronger enemies than Goliath. He had seen God come through before on various occasions. He could not be intimidated. He was not going to let these criticisms stop him. He refused to give in to them.

Never argue with your critics. It's a waste of time and energy. You can't win a race or a battle by spending your time focusing on the critics. You must be single-focused and refuse to give in. If criticism doesn't get on the inside of you, it has no effect on you.

It's only what takes residence on the inside of us that affects us. Criticisms are designed to get you sidetracked, off-pace, off-balance, and eventually defeated. Pay no attention to the critics. Keep your eyes on the road, prize and task ahead. If you do not give the critics or scoffers any focus and attention, you will win.

Speak Words Of Faith

And when the words were heard which David spoke, they rehearsed them before Saul: and he sent for him. And David said to Saul, Let no man's heart fail because of him; thy servant will go and fight with this Philistine.

— 1 Samuel 17:31-32

And David said unto Saul, Thy servant kept his father's sheep, and there came a lion, and a bear, and took a lamb out of the flock: And I went out after him, and smote him, and delivered it out of his mouth: and when he arose against me, I caught him by his beard, and smote him, and slew him. Thy servant slew both the lion and the bear: and this uncircumcised Philistine shall be as one of them, seeing he hath defied the armies of the living God. David said moreover, The LORD that delivered me out of the paw of the lion, and out of the paw of the bear, he will deliver me out of the hand of this Philistine. And Saul said unto David, Go, and the LORD be with thee.

— 1 Samuel 17:34-37

David was a man of faith. So much was done up to this point to try to bring him to fear and cause him to back down, but David did not give in or budge. He knew his God. He had seen Him come through several times. David responded in faith in this time of pressure and crisis. He never spoke any doubts or unbelief. **He never talked of what might not happen, but only what he believed would happen.** When everyone else who was experienced in war was in hiding, David boldly spoke forth his faith. David knew what he was doing and was laying groundwork for the battle ahead.

When you are preparing for battle, there is no time to think or speak your fears and negative thoughts, because if you do, you will get killed or defeated. You cannot even entertain the unbelief of people spewing negativity around you. And if you do, you must speak back and counter every single negative thing they say. You must speak forth faith and the promises of God. That's how you start to win.

Imagine what would have happened if David spoke his fears about Goliath. He would have been categorized the same as everyone else, and he would never have had a shot at taking down Goliath. He would have been dismissed just like everyone else. If David spoke like everyone else, we would never have heard of him as the giant slayer. It is important that you speak your faith and not doubt. People notice and pay attention to words of faith.

It is only because he spoke life, faith, and the promises of God that people around him noticed someone different was in their midst. They took his words before King Saul, and the king gave him a shot. Faith will get you to the top, but doubt, fear, and unbelief will cause you to sink.

The faith you speak will not go unnoticed; you will be challenged and confronted. Some people will try to shut you down because you are showing more courage than they are. The devil will always parade around you or have someone try to shut you up. Saul, Eliab, and Goliath all tried to shut David up and talk him out of his faith, but he overcame all of them.

For whatsoever is born of God overcometh the world: and this is the victory that overcometh the world, even our faith.

(1 John 5:4)

What are you speaking about your situation? Is it faith, or fears and doubt? Your victory could be determined by your confession because from the abundance of the heart the mouth speaks. What you speak reveals the condition of your heart.

Faith always has a testimony. David spoke forth his faith and then followed it up with a powerful testimony.

Rehearse Your Victories (Testimony)

And David said unto Saul, Thy servant kept his father's sheep, and there came a lion, and a bear, and took a lamb out of the flock: And I went out after him, and smote him, and delivered it out of his mouth: and when he arose against me, I caught him by his beard, and smote him, and slew him. Thy servant slew both the lion and the bear: and this uncircumcised Philistine shall be as one of them, seeing he hath defied the armies of the living God. David said moreover, The LORD that delivered me out of the paw of the lion, and out of the paw of the bear, he will deliver me out of the hand of this Philistine. And Saul said unto David, Go, and the LORD be with thee.

— 1 Samuel 17:34-37

You have a testimony. God has done something powerful in your life. What is it?

We need to look back in order to endure and face tomorrow. The victories we had, the giants we defeated, and all the good things God has done in the past can be used as the anchor for today and tomorrow.

David had seen God bring him through various challenges. He defeated a lion and a bear, and when the right time arose, he called this into memory. The reason was that since he had seen the faithfulness of God in the past, he could take on any enemies, including Goliath. David had dealt with much fiercer enemies (the lion and the bear). He was bold enough to take on any non-covenant man in the name of the Lord. The Lord had given him victory before, and He would give him victory again. If God did it in the past, He can do it again and even greater today. Never shy away from the victories God has wrought in your life (Psalm 40:5).

Faith is released when we remember, recall, and rehearse what God has done and what He has brought us through in the past.

Keep note of your victories and, in the time of need, call them to memory. You have to look back at God's faithfulness and your victories in order to move forward.

Humble Yourself

And Saul said to him, Whose son art thou, thou young man? And David answered, I am the son of thy servant Jesse the Bethlehemite.

— 1 Samuel 17:58

One of the greatest lessons we learn from David is humility. David was a uniquely humble young man. Knowing well he was anointed king over Israel, he continued to keep his father's sheep and remained subject to both his father and King Saul. There was a timing to which David would begin to ascend to the throne, but he did not become impatient.

We also see that when he went to speak to King Saul about this chance to obliterate the giant Goliath, David did not speak disrespectfully to King Saul, nor did he toot his own trumpet. We cannot see any disrespect towards the current king. A lesser man than David would have answered roughly, or made it known that he was the anointed one. He was humble and subject to King Saul. This is a tremendous example from David. He was not insecure at all, nor did he start to make things happen by calling all the shots.

Now, you might be thinking that David was just a young kid. He had no choice but to be subject to his father and Saul. You have to remember that he was the new anointed king, and he could have become arrogant, but he didn't.

The humility of David could be one of the reasons that King Saul entrusted his kingdom to a young shepherd boy. This was risky, but Saul did it, and I believe it had a lot to do with David's heart and attitude. King Saul also went on to bless David.

Our Strength is in The Lord

And David girded his sword upon his armor, and he assayed to go; for he had not proved it. And David said unto Saul, I cannot go with these; for I have not proved them. And David put them off him.

— 1 Samuel 17:39

King Saul wanted to give his armor to David, but after David tried it on, he realized it was not going to work. Our strength is not in our wisdom, armor, or in physical things, but in the Lord. This is not to say that we can't use weapons or body armor, but we must keep our trust and dependency in the Lord—not in physical things like men or weapons. These things have their right place, use and value, but not as replacements for faith, dependence and trust in God.

Saul was trying to have David use the very armor that did not work for him. Why do people like to give advice that they themselves cannot use or that does not work for them? When they see how resilient you are in what you stand for, they stop opposing you and resort to offering some sort of advice that they can't even use themselves.

David had refused being talked out of fighting Goliath, but then when Saul figured he could not convince him, and that David would not give in nor back down, he offered his useless armor. But David was smart enough to turn it down and know that his victory was not going to come because of Saul's armor. His strength was in the Lord, not in anything physical. He also had not tried or proved this armor, but had tried the faithfulness of the Lord and His strength.

David was not afraid to believe God and go without the armor. He had seen victories without it and was going to see another without wearing Saul's useless armor. Praise the Lord! He was right. He stunned Goliath and all the Philistines.

> *The horse is prepared against the day of battle: but safety is of the LORD.*
>
> — Proverbs 21:31

> *Some trust in chariots, and some in horses: but we will remember the name of the LORD our God.*
>
> — Psalm 20:7

Stick with What Has Worked in the Past

> *And David girded his sword upon his armor, and he attempted to go; for he had not proved it. And David said unto Saul, I cannot go with these; for I have not proved them. And David put them off him. And he took his staff in his hand, and chose him five smooth stones out of the brook, and put them in a shepherd's bag which he had, even in a scrip; and his sling was in his hand: and he drew near to the Philistine.*
>
> — 1 Samuel 17:39-40

David had never used a sword or armor. This was the wrong time to try! A lesser person would have been so fearful that they would have forced themselves to use this armor, but not David. David was so secure in trusting and depending on the Lord that he would still fight without the armor.

He knew that victory came not by the physical, but by the Lord. David quickly realized that it was not going to work for him. He said, "I have not proved nor tried this armor. I can't use it."

David stuck to what he knew, what he had proved, and what had worked before in the past—his dependence upon God.

David was not going to just fight Goliath—he was going to fight until he won. He was going to persevere. I think this is the reason he took up five stones, although he was fighting only one man. He was ready to draw another stone if one was not sufficient to annihilate this giant. He was going to go hard after him and utterly destroy him. David had proven this style and was comfortable with it, but his trust was still in the Lord and not in his sling and stone. How do we know? He said it. He said that Goliath was up against God, not David. He said the battle was the Lord's. Dependence on the Lord had worked for him big-time, and he was not going to abandon it for something else.

Many of us have seen God come through in the past on our behalf by putting faith in Him, but now we are trying to put trust in man, in weapons, in armor, and so forth. We need to stick to what we have proven—reliance upon God alone.

Speak Back—
Counter The Negative Words

And the Philistine said to David, Come to me, and I will give thy flesh unto the fowls of the air, and to the beasts of the field.

— 1 Samuel 17:44

We should never underestimate the power of words—positive or negative. Life and death is in the power of the tongue—our words (Proverbs 23:7). Words have the power to bring forth life or to bring forth death. We should never take this lightly.

Goliath despised and criticized David because he was a shepherd with no "experience." He had no idea he was up against an anointed king. Had he known who he was up against, he probably would not have shown up to fight.

Goliath spewed all his negative words to instill fear in David, but David was not going to stand there and let those negative words take root in him. What did he do? He spoke back like a fire hose.

Then said David to the Philistine, Thou comest to me with a sword, and with a spear, and with a shield: but I come to thee in the name of the LORD of hosts, the God of the armies of Israel, whom thou hast defied. This day will the LORD deliver thee into mine hand; and I will smite thee, and take thine head from thee; and I will give the carcasses of the host of the Philistines this day unto the fowls of the air, and to the wild beasts of the earth; that all the earth may know that there is a God in Israel. And all this assembly shall know that the LORD saveth not with sword and spear: for the battle is the LORD's, and he will give you into our hands.

— 1 Samuel 17:45-47

He spoke more than what Goliath anticipated. He was not going to retreat. He countered and spoke forth his faith and what he was going to do to him.

David was never afraid. I strongly believe that the words we do not counter affect us and they hardly leave our subconscious mind. They keep coming back time and again, and I think that is one of the reasons we must counter any negative words spoken against us. If David had not spoken back and left those words to linger over him, they would have instilled fear into his heart. This is the lesson we must learn from this fearless shepherd!

The Unfair Fight—The Battle Is The Lord's

Then said David to the Philistine, Thou comest to me with a sword, and with a spear, and with a shield: but I come to thee in the name of the LORD of hosts, the God of the armies of Israel, whom thou hast defied. This day will the LORD deliver thee into mine hand; and I will smite thee, and take thine head from thee; and I will give the carcasses of the host of the Philistines this day unto the fowls of the air, and to the wild beasts of the earth; that all the earth may know that there is a God in Israel. And all this assembly shall know that the LORD saveth not with sword and spear: for the battle is the LORD's, and he will give you into our hands. And it came to pass, when the Philistine arose, and came and drew nigh to meet David, that David hasted, and ran toward the army to meet the Philistine. And David put his hand in his bag, and took thence a stone, and slung it, and smote the Philistine in his forehead, that the stone sunk into his forehead; and he fell upon his face to the earth. So David prevailed over the Philistine with a sling and with a stone, and smote the Philistine, and slew him; but there was no sword in the hand of David. Therefore David ran, and stood upon the Philistine, and took his sword, and drew it out of the sheath thereof, and slew him, and cut off his head therewith. And when the Philistines saw their champion was dead, they fled.

— 1 Samuel 17:45-51

This fight was not fair. Goliath was up against God, but he did not believe that. David revealed clearly that he came against Goliath in the name of the Lord of hosts, the God of the armies of Israel.

Goliath was focused on the physical, or outward, appearance of David, but he had no idea that this was an anointed king. He thought this was just a young shepherd boy.

David was small in stature and insignificant in his outward appearance, but he was a million times bigger than Goliath on the inside because God was with him. One person with God is a majority. God was the one going to fight, not David. He was going to fight through the willingness of David. It's important to remember that God works through people. We are the medium He has chosen.

When we experience victory in our lives, we should always remember that it was not us, but God who was working through us (Philippians 2:13). This keeps us from being caught up in pride. We know we did not do it. If you can do things in your own power and strength, without depending on God's help, then you have missed God big-time. If you think you have arrived without being dependent on God, you have not arrived. If God is not the reason for your victory, if He is not the subject of your success, you have missed God.

Goliath had no chance against David. He could not win this fight. He agreed to fight the wrong kid. Goliath would have been better off fighting another giant that did not know God or have a covenant with Him than to fight a kid who knew God and had a covenant with Him. His chances of winning would have been tremendously higher.

I remember when I was young and I heard of this battle between David and Goliath, it never clicked that David won because God was on his side. I thought David won because he was small and somehow was able to beat the giant bully.

God being on David's side is what made the difference.

Regardless of how big your enemy or giant is, the Lord Jesus is with you, and you can win. You can overcome. You can defeat that giant in your life.

One is a majority when God is with him. Never give up trusting the Lord because He can write victory in your life beyond your wildest imagination; however, we must cooperate with God; speak forth your faith and then act on it.

You are a winner—a victor by default. Do not give up your ground of default victory. Anyone up against you, any problem, and any disease is up against the Lord.

Completely Annihilate and Obliterate Your Enemy

Therefore David ran, and stood upon the Philistine, and took his sword, and drew it out of the sheath thereof, and slew him, and cut off his head therewith. And when the Philistines saw their champion was dead, they fled.

— 1 Samuel 17:51

David wasn't taking any chances. Goliath could only have been knocked out or slipped and fallen. David had to go ahead and finish the fight. He ran and took Goliath's sword and cut off his head. He completely destroyed his enemy and left no stone unturned. He also raised the head of Goliath, after which the Philistine army began to flee. They were waiting to see if their champion had been completely killed. Raising his head took away any doubts.

It is not enough to just knock out your giants or just chase your enemies around the corner and then stop. You must completely obliterate all your enemies so that they never have to appear or rise again. By faith in the Lord and complete trust in Him, you can utterly wipe out all your enemies and giants. Do not settle for partial victory, but full victory. You can beat cancer, you can beat HIV and AIDS, and you can completely attain victory in any area of your life. The Lord is with you.

Fear Not

And it came to pass, when the Philistine arose, and came and drew nigh to meet David, that David hasted, and ran toward the army to meet the Philistine.

— 1 Samuel 17:48

If God is not with us, we have every cause to fear. But that is not the case. God is with us; and therefore, we should not be afraid—our enemies should. David understood this very well, and he said so as he went up to take on Goliath. David was a fearless man. I also believe that this did not come overnight. As he walked with the Lord on a daily basis, and as he saw the miracles and wonders God wrought on his behalf, he grew in confidence and trust towards the Lord. David had been seeking God for quite some time, even while he was still a young man. His heart was fixed on the Lord (Psalm 57:7). Proverbs 28:1 says that, "The wicked flee when no man pursueth: but the righteous are bold as a lion." David was bold as a lion because he was in covenant and right standing with God.

When the time came to go head-to-head with Goliath,

David ran towards him. He did not retreat, but took the offensive. But why was this young boy so bold? He had a covenant with God, and so do you. David had seen God do greater victories in his life, like when he killed the bear and lion; and so have you. David believed and knew the Lord was with him. Do you? David knew and believed the battle was the Lord's. Do you? David was anointed and so are you. He also prepared his heart to seek the Lord before this crisis. He did so in advance. Have you?

You Have A Part To Play

And he took his staff in his hand, and chose him five smooth stones out of the brook, and put them in a shepherd's bag which he had, even in a scrip; and his sling was in his hand: and he drew near to the Philistine. And the Philistine came on and drew near unto David; and the man that bore the shield went before him. And when the Philistine looked about, and saw David, he disdained him: for he was but a youth, and ruddy, and of a fair countenance. And the Philistine said unto David, Am I a dog, that thou comest to me with staves? And the Philistine cursed David by his gods. And the Philistine said to David, Come to me, and I will give thy flesh unto the fowls of the air, and to the beasts of the field. Then said David to the Philistine, Thou comest to me with a sword, and with a spear, and with a shield: but I come to thee in the name of the LORD of hosts, the God of the armies of Israel, whom thou hast defied. This day will the LORD deliver thee into mine hand; and I will smite thee, and take thine head from thee; and I will give the carcasses of the host of the Philistines this day unto the fowls of the air, and to the wild beasts of the earth; that all the earth may know that there is a God in Israel. And all this assembly shall know that the LORD saveth not with sword and spear: for the battle is the LORD's, and he will give you into our hands. And it came to pass, when the Philistine arose, and came and drew nigh to meet David, that David hasted, and ran toward the army to meet the Philistine. And David put his hand in his bag, and took thence a stone, and slung it, and smote the Philistine in his forehead, that the stone sunk into his forehead; and he fell upon his face to the earth. So David prevailed over the Philistine with a sling and with a stone, and smote the Philistine, and slew him; but there was no sword in the hand of David. Therefore David ran, and stood upon the Philistine, and took his sword, and drew it out of the sheath thereof, and slew him, and cut off his head therewith. And when the Philistines saw their champion was dead, they fled.

— 1 Samuel 17:40-51

Many people believe that God is so sovereign that He can do anything without us. This is not true: God is so sovereign that He chose not to do certain things without us. God works through people; therefore, we have a part to play. David believed God, but did not stay home. Faith without works is dead (James 2:17). If you truly believe something, your actions will correspond with what you believe. True faith will have corresponding actions. David showed up to do what he could do, so that God could do what only He alone can do.

David was not a man of cheap talk. He was a man of action. He spoke forth his faith and he then acted on it. Now that's faith! He took his sling, his staff, and his five stones. He countered the trash talk from the enemy, ran toward Goliath, took a stone and slung it, and continued on to cut off the head of Goliath the Philistine. This was all faith being displayed by David. David believed and acted.

Everything David did, he saw it on the inside of him before he could do it. You must see it on the inside, before you can see it on the outside. If you can't see it on the inside you will not see it on the outside. David believed every word he said and acted accordingly. You can see his faith by his actions. Can your faith be seen by your actions? If you truly believe something, you can't help but act accordingly.

Do not be passive—step out in active faith. To kill a giant, you must go up and fight him. To walk on water, you must get out of the boat. To see people healed, you must pray and lay hands on the sick. Do something in faith—learn from David.

The Enemy In Your Life Is Afraid Of You

And Saul was afraid of David, because the LORD was with him, and was departed from Saul.

— 1 Samuel 18:12

Saul started to persecute David once he realized that he had become a threat to his throne. After David killed Goliath and the women began to sing, "Saul has killed thousands, but David ten thousands", King Saul was not pleased and got very angry. He started to hunt for David's life; however, David behaved wisely because he knew Saul was trying to kill him.

Because David behaved wisely, and his behavior was spot-on in that he never gave Saul a reason or a loophole by his actions, Saul became even more afraid of David.

Our actions and behavior also play a major part in whether our enemies will be afraid of us. We should not give the enemy a chance or reason not to be afraid of us. We should live godly lives, which in return, will fend off most of our enemies. Romans 6:16 says, *"Know ye not, that to whom ye yield yourselves servants to obey, his servants ye are to whom ye obey; whether of sin unto death, or of obedience unto righteousness?"*

Saul could not find blemish in David's life, and David gave him no reason to do so. David escaped Saul's first attempt to kill him with a javelin and also multiple other attempts. After David avoided these attempts, it was clear to Saul that the Lord was with David. Every time he tried, he failed, but it was mainly because David stayed sensitive to the Lord and the Lord tipped him off. He saw what was coming before the enemy executed his plan, and he was able to slip out of the enemy's jaws.

It's critical to understand that there is no record that David was ever afraid of Saul. Even though he ran multiple times for his life, it was not an indication that he was fearful, but that he was very smart and wise.

However, the scriptures clearly spell out that Saul was afraid of David. Saul was afraid of him because the Lord was with him.

This is true for all of the enemies in our lives. They are afraid of us because they know that God is with us. Diseases, sickness, poverty, and so forth are enemies that have already been defeated. Although they might try to attack, they are totally afraid of us because God is with us. Therefore, we can retain our position of victory, take our God-given authority, and fear not.

Since David was never afraid of Saul, we should not be afraid of any of our enemies either. On the contrary, they should be afraid of us because God Almighty, the Creator of the heavens and Earth, is with us.

Do Not Quit

And Saul cast the javelin; for he said, I will smite David even to the wall with it. And David avoided out of his presence twice.

— 1 Samuel 18:11

We should learn to develop thick skin in that we do not give up nor quit. Saul wanted to kill David, and David knew it, but he was called to serve King Saul, and it was very premature for him to quit.

The threat on David's life would have been enough for most people. They would have quit, but not David. David knew he was in the right place despite the persecution. I wonder what would have become of David had he quit due to persecution, because days later, Saul *"removed him from him"* (1 Samuel 18:13) and made him captain over a thousand men and he went out and came in before the people. He started to gain favor with the people (1 Samuel 18:16). This was another step towards his future kingdom and reign.

Still, Saul tried to kill him multiple times, but David was smart and avoided Saul's presence more than twice. Most people would not put up with the first attempt, let alone the second and third. David, however, was as faithful as he had been with his father's sheep.

The lion and the bear came to steal his sheep, but David did not quit and slew them. This shows the thick skin David had. If someone can take on a lion and bear, he can handle persecution from Saul. If you do not quit, then your adversary or enemy will. We have to be sensitive to the leading of the Lord. Sometimes you don't have to carry your bag and leave because this and that has happened, or is happening. "What is God saying?" is the question to answer regardless of how obvious the decision might be. Usually you can determine if you are on track by whether there is any persecution. We should never quit when being persecuted. It means that we are on track because all who live godly lives shall suffer persecution (2 Timothy 3:12).

There came a time when David had to move on, but it was not his immediate and upfront decision. I don't consider that quitting. It's moving on. In 1 Samuel 19:9-10, David fled for his life again. So, there came a point to resign or move on, but it wasn't the very first thing David did. He served faithfully even with his life was in constant danger. We can learn so much from David.

An Offer from An Enemy — Is It Worth Taking?

And Saul said to David, Behold my elder daughter Merab, her will I give thee to wife: only be thou valiant for me, and fight the LORD's battles. For Saul said, Let not mine hand be upon him, but let the hand of the Philistines be upon him. And David said unto Saul, Who am I? and what is my life, or my father's family in Israel, that I should be son-in-law to the king? But it came to pass at the time when Merab Saul's daughter should have been given to David, that she was given unto Adriel the Meholathite to wife.

— 1 Samuel 18:17-19

David was Saul's enemy, but Saul was not David's enemy. David had seen the earlier dealings of Saul and how he wanted to kill him. Now, this same enemy shows up with an offer for David to marry his daughter, but the offer was not genuine. It was designed to trap and kill David. Notice, David did not jump at the offer even though it logically looked like it would accelerate his ascension to the throne. This was a shortcut from the enemy (Saul) who was trying to kill David. David was humble and smart. He asked why he had chosen him to marry her. He clearly stated that he was a nobody, neither was his family. Was it worth David taking this sleazy offer?

Still, David accepted the offer and he was engaged to Merab, but Saul had different plans. He pulled an evil trick on David and took Merab and gave her away to another man. Saul wanted to hurt David, although it looks like Merab was hurt by this more than David. What Saul meant to destroy David ended up devastating his own daughter even more. It's quite clear that Saul never cared about his daughter, and he loved himself more than anyone else.

David could well have thought that Saul was setting a trap for him. This offer was not worth even considering, because it was all set up from the day King Saul recognized that God was with David and that he was a threat to his kingdom. Even the second offer of Saul's daughter Michal was designed to get David killed as he went out to get the foreskins of the Philistines. But because God was with David, God tuned the thing that was meant to destroy him into one more of David's victories. What a resume! An offer from a sleazeball ball is not worth consideration.

Very Present Help In Time Of Need

And Saul spoke to Jonathan his son, and to all his servants, that they should kill David. But Jonathan Saul's son delighted much in David: and Jonathan told David, saying, Saul my father seeketh to kill thee: now therefore, I pray thee, take heed to thyself until the morning, and abide in a secret place, and hide thyself: And I will go out and stand beside my father in the field where thou art, and I will commune with my father of thee; and what I see, that I will tell thee. And Jonathan spoke good of David unto Saul his father, and said unto him, Let not the king sin against his servant, against David; because he hath not sinned against thee, and because his works have been to thee-ward very good: For he did put his life in his hand, and slew the Philistine, and the LORD wrought a great salvation for all Israel: thou sawest it, and didst rejoice: wherefore then wilt thou sin against innocent blood, to slay David without a cause? And Saul hearkened unto the voice of Jonathan: and Saul swore, As the LORD liveth, he shall not be slain.

— 1 Samuel 19:1-6

David's life was in trouble, although every trap and plan Saul had set to kill David fell flat. In these verses, we see that he ordered all his servants and his son Jonathan to kill David. David had just slaughtered the Philistines and brought back their foreskins at King Saul's request as dowry for his wife-to-be, but all of this was designed to get him killed. Had it not been for God, who was continually with him, he might not have escaped death (1 Samuel 21:8-9).

This intensified Saul's desire to kill David, but God had a godly man, a friend to David, who tipped him off. Jonathan was the man that God worked through to protect and preserve David's life once again. He was David's advocate before Saul. He spoke reason and godliness into Saul's head, asking why he wanted to kill David, all the while pleading David's case. Had it not been for Jonathan, God's very present help in this time of need, things would have been different.

Regardless of what you are going through, God is readily present, just as He was for David through Jonathan. Just call upon Him and He will answer you and deliver you. He is not present to see you suffer, but to bring you comfort and deliverance (Isaiah 43:1-2).

Jonathan was putting his life on the line to defend and protect David, but it was only because he loved David as his own soul, and he was a godly man who saw things with a godly perspective. He knew that God was with David, but he was also defending the very man who would displace him as the next king in line after Saul. Jonathan put David ahead of himself. What a godly example and godly man Jonathan was! What a man of integrity. The truth is that God has a Jonathan for you, too.

Jonathan loved David not just in word, but in action. He did not keep his love concealed in fear of Saul, but when he saw his friend in trouble, he stepped up, defended and helped him. True love stands up and fights against those who hurt the very ones we love, including the Lord (John 15:13). The entire defense that Jonathan mounted for David was nothing but God protecting David in the very time of need.

Michal, David's new wife, was also used of God to help warn David and send him off before Saul's men came to kill him. Again, God was very present through Michal protecting David from his enemy, Saul. God's protection is more than enough, and He is readily present to help in your time of need.

God's Will – A Bed Of Roses? Challenges Will Still Come

And David arose, and fled that day for fear of Saul, and went to Achish the king of Gath.

— 1 Samuel 21:10

And he changed his behavior before them, and feigned himself mad in their hands, and scrabbled on the doors of the gate, and let his spittle fall down upon his beard.

— 1 Samuel 21:13

David was called and anointed by God to be King over Israel, but the days and years following his anointing were years of flight. He fled for his life on a daily basis. It looked like he would never be king. It was difficult to the point that he had to play a mad man just to save his life (1 Samuel 21:11-15). Who could have imagined that a man anointed to be king would have to do such a thing? Who could have imagined that the same man would later go and dwell with the people of Goliath just to save his neck from Saul?

These were very challenging times for David, for he had to stay focused and keep his God-birthed vision alive and not give up. Giving up would not have made it come to pass, but holding on and enduring could and did. He had to persevere. His family was in trouble because he was chosen to be king, and therefore a threat to another man's throne. Lots of people died in the process due to Saul's insecurity (1 Samuel 22:17-18). Nothing came easily for David to finally take the throne. God's will is not automatic and surely not a bed of roses. There will be challenges and hardships, but be of good cheer. We have overcome! If we do not give up, if we do not quit, we will see God's will come to pass no matter the challenges, hardships, and persecution we endure. Although it tarries, wait for it, it shall come (Habakkuk 2:3).

Seek and Inquire Of The Lord

Therefore David inquired of the LORD, saying, Shall I go and smite these Philistines? And the LORD said unto David, Go, and smite the Philistines, and save Keilah. And David's men said unto him, Behold, we be afraid here in Judah: how much more then if we come to Keilah against the armies of the Philistines? Then David inquired of the LORD yet again. And the LORD answered him and said, Arise, go down to Keilah; for I will deliver the Philistines into thine hand.

— 1 Samuel 23:2-4

David had over four hundred men that had joined themselves to him as he continued to flee from Saul. A time arose where David had to make some decisions, but he did not just jump to make them. He first went and inquired of the Lord. Notice that this was during the most difficult time of David's life. He did not just do what he felt was good, but he went and asked the Lord.

David was still God-dependent even during a time of stress, crisis, danger, and turmoil. We should learn the same lesson: not to act out of distress or pressure, but go and hear from the Lord first before we take any steps forward.

We need to develop a habit of inquiring of the Lord in our decision-making. David is a good example of this characteristic. Although he did not do it all of the time, there are times where he continually sought the Lord before making any major decision. For more examples of this, read 1 Samuel 23:2-4 and 1 Samuel 30:8.

Will You Take A Shortcut?

And the men of David said unto him, Behold the day of which the LORD said unto thee, Behold, I will deliver thine enemy into thine hand, that thou mayest do to him as it shall seem good unto thee. Then David arose, and cut off the skirt of Saul's robe privily.

— 1 Samuel 24:4

After Saul continually sought to kill David from place to place, an opportunity for David to kill Saul presented itself. What an opportunity to be king the very next day! A lesser man than David would have taken this opportunity to do evil to Saul, but David would not. David was willing to wait as long as it took for God to elevate him to kingship. He was not going to take any shortcut or kick down any doors in order to make God's call come to pass in his life. This portrays David's heart. David's heart was right. He only wanted to become king because God had chosen him. He refused to kill Saul in order to ascend to the throne.

David was trusting in the Lord to make things happen. David refused to kill the very person that sought to kill him on multiple occasions. We should never make God's will come to pass through our own strength and abilities. We should remain God-dependent and refuse any shortcuts. Shortcuts are of the devil. If God gets you there, He will keep you there, but if you get yourself there, you will have to compromise to keep yourself there. Let God do it for you. This is a great lesson.

This was some serious temptation for David to overcome. He was able to overcome because his heart was prepared ahead of time to seek the Lord. He had made decisions in advance so that when opportunity showed up, he did not take that shortcut. He also had been seeking the Lord and had his heart continually sensitive towards God and hardened towards what was wrong. If David's heart was hardened towards God like King Saul's, he would never have been convicted or smote at heart for cutting off the skirt of Saul's robe privily (1 Samuel 24:4).

Vengeance Is Of The Lord

Behold, this day thine eyes have seen how that the LORD had delivered thee today into mine hand in the cave: and some bade me kill thee: but mine eye spared thee; and I said, I will not put forth mine hand against my lord; for he is the LORD's anointed. Moreover, my father, see, yea, see the skirt of thy robe in my hand: for in that I cut off the skirt of thy robe, and killed thee not, know thou and see that there is neither evil nor transgression in mine hand, and I have not sinned against thee; yet thou huntest my soul to take it. The LORD judge between me and thee, and the LORD avenge me of thee: but mine hand shall not be upon thee.

— 1 Samuel 24:10-12

The LORD therefore be judge, and judge between me and thee, and see, and plead my cause, and deliver me out of thine hand.

— 1 Samuel 24:15

Another life lesson we learn from the life of David is that he refused to take vengeance into his own hands. He had an opportunity to kill Saul, but he refused to take justice or revenge into his own hands. All the people would have sided with David had he killed Saul, but he was not looking for the approval and the praise of men. **We can and should still act correctly even when we are hurting and in pain.**

David had tremendous respect for the anointing of God upon King Saul's life. He respected the office that Saul held.

A lesser man than David would have taken vengeance into his own hands, but true vengeance is the Lord's (Romans 12:17-19). If we take vengeance into our own hands, we do a very poor job; but if we let God do it, He does a fantastic job. David refused to recompense evil for evil, but he chose to recompense evil for good (Romans 12:21). If David, a man in the lesser covenant, was able to turn the other cheek, we, under the new covenant, the better covenant, can do the same.

Respect For Office

And he said unto his men, The LORD forbid that I should do this thing unto my master, the LORD's anointed, to stretch forth mine hand against him, seeing he is the anointed of the LORD.

— 1 Samuel 24:6

David had a tremendous respect for Saul; not just for Saul, but for the office he held as well. This was one of the reasons David refused to kill him, even when he had multiple opportunities. He said that he would not stretch forth his hand against the anointed of the Lord.

I can't think of a lot of people who have regard for the office or position that is held by someone they disagree with. We live in a culture where we are trained not to have regard for anyone in any position when they are wrong. This has promoted continuous rebellion towards different offices of leadership.

Here, we learn a life lesson that we should continue to honor the office and the person that is holding it, even if they are wrong or if we disagree with them. We should not only honor the office when the leader is doing everything right, but even when he is doing wrong. David's men had the mentality that many people have, but not David. They wanted Saul dead, but David as a leader inspired them to repent and see things the way he did.

David let Saul get away. He let him off the hook. How many people would do that?

Trusting The Lord

The LORD judge between me and thee, and the LORD avenge me of thee: but mine hand shall not be upon thee.

— 1 Samuel 24:12

David was a man who trusted the Lord. It took more faith for David not to kill Saul than to kill Goliath. David was a man of war. It would have been easier for him to slaughter Saul. This was not a simple decision for David and I believe it was challenging.

It's time to let God be the judge. David refused to promote himself, but trusted God to do so. Psalm 75:6-7 says, *"For promotion cometh neither from the east, nor from the west, nor from the south. But God is the judge: he putteth down one, and setteth up another."* Very few people would have taken the high road David took. Few would have swam against the current, but David waited for God to promote him. To David, the means justified the end, but to most people, the end justifies the means. What a sorry position to hold. We must learn from David.

People Can Tell When You Are Anointed

I pray thee, forgive the trespass of thine handmaid: for the LORD will certainly make my lord a sure house; because my lord fighteth the battles of the LORD, and evil hath not been found in thee all thy days. Yet a man is risen to pursue thee, and to seek thy soul: but the soul of my lord shall be bound in the bundle of life with the LORD thy God; and the souls of thine enemies, them shall he sling out, as out of the middle of a sling. And it shall come to pass, when the LORD shall have done to my lord according to all the good that he hath spoken concerning thee, and shall have appointed thee ruler over Israel;That this shall be no grief unto thee, nor offense of heart unto my lord, either that thou hast shed blood causeless, or that my lord hath avenged himself: but when the LORD shall have dealt well with my lord, then remember thine handmaid.

— 1 Samuel 25:28-31

How did Abigail know David was the chosen ruler over Israel? How did she know about all of the persecution? When Samuel anointed David to be king after Saul, David's family never told anyone that David was to be king in Saul's place. For one thing, it would have cost them their lives. Insecure Saul would have killed them all, but as time went by, people in Israel started to see something different about David. Many believed that he was going to become king in Saul's place. God had chosen David and confirmed this to the people without David saying a word. Saul knew David was to be king in his place, which birthed his desire to kill him, but the people could not be fooled because they knew David was to be the next king in line. They knew David was God's chosen. They saw the anointing of God upon David as the next chosen King of Israel.

The lesson we can learn here is that, if God has called and chosen you, He will convince and confirm it to the people. You do not have to toot your own horn or publicize it because the people can see it. Anointing cannot be hidden. It is visible and people can tell. People know who is anointed and who is not. They know who is chosen and who is faking it. Are you chosen and called of God?

Can An Oath Or Curse Be Reversed?

Now David had said, Surely in vain have I kept all that this fellow hath in the wilderness, so that nothing was missed of all that pertained unto him: and he hath requited me evil for good. So and more also do God unto the enemies of David, if I leave of all that pertain to him by the morning light any that pisseth against the wall.

— 1 Samuel 25:21-22

David made a blunder here. He made an oath that he was going to destroy all the males of Nabal's house, but he did not keep that oath. He also pronounced a curse upon himself in the heat of the moment. This would have had some serious repercussion on David's part, but he did something that changed the curse had he failed to fulfill the oath he had made.

Making this oath was not a smart thing for David to do, but when he was challenged by Abigail not to do the evil he had planned to do, David was quick to recognize her wisdom and repented of those foolish plans. David's repentance and desire to do what was right after he saw that he was wrong voided the curse and the oath. If we do not continue to do what is wrong and repent from it, God doesn't hold us accountable for the oaths, curses and vows we have spoken. To repent means to change the way we think, not necessarily the way we act. It's after we change the way we think that we can change the way we act. Our behavior is a result of our thinking patterns (Proverbs 23:6-7). It all starts by changing our thinking.

Be Consistent

Now David had said, Surely in vain have I kept all that this fellow hath in the wilderness, so that nothing was missed of all that pertained unto him: and he hath requited me evil for good. So and more also do God unto the enemies of David, if I leave of all that pertain to him by the morning light any that pisseth against the wall.

— 1 Samuel 25:21-22

It's staggering to think that David wanted to destroy Nabal for not giving his men food, even if he had protected them and all their flocks (1 Samuel 25:15-16). He said that Nabal was rewarding him evil for good. Earlier, we saw a David who was dependent on God and never took vengeance into his own hands when it came to Saul—he let God do it. But here he was considering killing Nabal, an evil man. Yet he was not willing to do so to a man who was hunting him for his life. This was hypocritical and inconsistent.

What Nabal did was very trivial in comparison to what Saul did. Saul was a bigger threat to David by far, yet David spared his life on multiple occasions, but he wanted to kill Nabal for bread. Something is wrong with this picture. If he would not avenge himself on Saul, he should not avenge himself on Nabal (1 Samuel 25:17). He should have let God do so, and to David's credit he eventually did, and God avenged him (1 Samuel 25:38). We have to be consistent in trusting God and depending on Him. We cannot pick and choose when and in what to trust God. We must be consistent.

Do Not Multiply Wives

David also took Ahinoam of Jezreel; and they were also both of them his wives.

— 1 Samuel 25:43

And David took him more concubines and wives out of Jerusalem, after he was come from Hebron: and there were yet sons and daughters born to David.

— 2 Samuel 5:13

Sexual problems were one of David's major weaknesses. David missed it in this area, stupendously. He was beginning to slip away. How could he have missed what Deuteronomy 17:17 taught? Marrying Abigail was understandable since her husband Nabal had died. And Saul had given Michal, his first wife, to another man — Phalti son of Laish. But when David took on Ahinoam of Jezreel as his wife, he broke the command God had given specifically for kings. This brought trouble into David's life as Ahinoam gave birth to Amon, who later committed incest with his half-sister Tamar and was later killed by her brother Absalom (2 Samuel 3:2 and 2 Samuel 13).

David was no exception to this command, and we can only suppose why he did this. I am pretty sure this was lust that was starting to creep into his life. These multiple wives—eight in total (2 Samuel 3:2-5)—started to turn his heart away from fully following the Lord, which led to his adultery with Bathsheba. Who knows, but David's accumulation of more wives and concubines (2 Samuel 5:13) could have encouraged Solomon having hundreds of wives.

We should guard our hearts in every aspect because a little crack will invite the enemy in. God knew well why He forbade them from having multiple wives, and going against His instructions was not a smart idea. We should also learn to hearken to God's Word. Our position of authority doesn't exempt us from obedience.

Encourage Yourself In The Lord

And it came to pass, when David and his men were come to Ziklag on the third day, that the Amalekites had invaded the south, and Ziklag, and smitten Ziklag, and burned it with fire; And had taken the women captives, that were therein: they slew not any, either great or small, but carried them away, and went on their way. So David and his men came to the city, and, behold, it was burned with fire; and their wives, and their sons, and their daughters, were taken captives. Then David and the people that were with him lifted up their voice and wept, until they had no more power to weep. And David's two wives were taken captives, Ahinoam the Jezreelitess, and Abigail the wife of Nabal the Carmelite. And David was greatly distressed; for the people spoke of stoning him, because the soul of all the people was grieved, every man for his sons and for his daughters: but David encouraged himself in the LORD his God. And David said to Abiathar the priest, Ahimelech's son, I pray thee, bring me hither the ephod. And Abiathar brought thither the ephod to David. And David inquired at the LORD, saying, Shall I pursue after this troop? Shall I overtake them? And he answered him, Pursue: for thou shalt surely overtake them, and without fail recover all.

— 1 Samuel 30:1-8

At this time, David was living with the Philistines and was given his own city called Ziklag, where he dwelt by

King Achish. David rose in the morning to go fight with the Philistines as asked by King Achish because they had gathered their armies for war against Israel; however, this displeased the lords of King Achish. They worried that David would not fight with them, but would instead turn and fight against them. Therefore, they asked the king to have David and his men return to their city, Ziklag.

When they arrived back at Ziklag, they found turmoil. They had been invaded by the Amalekites and the city had been burned with fire. All their belongings, including their children, their wives, and their cattle had been taken captive by the Amalekites. It was a sad day and discouragement arose among David's men to the point that they wept until they could weep no more. David was distressed, grieved, and discouraged, and the men who were with him were so indignant that they spoke of stoning him. His life was in danger once again, not by Saul, but by his very men.

But, David encouraged himself in the Lord. Instead of sitting there and discouraged forever, David decided to encourage himself in the Lord. He asked for the ephod to be brought to him, which would be the equivalent of God's Word. David read it and inquired of the Lord whether to pursue, the Amalekites. God told him to go ahead and pursue for he would overtake them.

It is worth taking note of how David responded. He encouraged himself in the Lord. He did not call or wait for someone else to come and encourage him. Most people would have done the very opposite, but not David. He took responsibility for encouraging himself. We should do the same. He took the initiative to do so even as a leader. **Once you become a leader, you should be willing to give up your right to be discouraged or have a bad day.** You are the one to motivate and inspire others to action, and your discouragement won't help.

David then asked for God's Word. Why? He drew his encouragement and instruction from it. We should always refer to the Word of God for encouragement and instruction. After David had read the Word, he got an answer on the next step to take, which was to pursue and go after the Amalekites.

It is your responsibility to encourage yourself in the Lord, not anyone else's. Find a way to motivate yourself into action. Get off your couch, get out of bed, stop the pity-party and encourage yourself in the Lord, after which you will get clear direction on how to proceed.

Notice also that direction and instruction came only after he had encouraged himself in the Lord. We must take certain steps to begin to see certain things change. The other thing we can learn is to never fall into self-pity and quit because of a tragedy we have faced. Imagine if David had fallen into depression or had given up. He was just hours away from becoming king in Saul's place. His breakthrough and fulfillment of his dreams was just around the corner. Do not quit (1 Corinthians 10:13), because if you don't, you will eventually win. Your breakthrough is nearer than it has ever been. It's just a matter of time.

Someone Must Take Responsibility For This. Whose Fault Is It? Who Is To Blame?

And it came to pass, when David and his men were come to Ziklag on the third day, that the Amalekites had invaded the south, and Ziklag, and smitten Ziklag, and burned it with fire; And had taken the women captives, that were therein: they slew not any, either great or small, but carried them away, and went on their way. So David and his men came to the city, and, behold, it was burned with fire; and their wives, and their sons, and their daughters, were taken captives.

— 1 Samuel 30:1-3

What a tragedy this was, and the logical questions would be, "Why did this happen and whose fault was it?"

First, I have to say that I believe that it was not the Lord who caused this tragedy to happen. David had a lot of blame in this happening, not God. David had raided the Amalekites earlier, and this could have been revenge on their part. The Amalekites knew of the Philistines preparing to go to war, and they took advantage of this time to pay them back, especially to the city of Ziklag, where David lived.

This also begs another question: Why did David leave the city and leave all their families and belongings defenseless? He took all the men with him. This was not a smart decision. David's collaboration with the Philistines could have caused this tragedy, and/or Saul's failure to completely wipe out these Amalekites (1 Samuel 15).

God had nothing to do with this. Also, I must say that David was not operating in God's perfect will. If God was behind this, then why would He not have the wives and children of David and all his men killed? Why would He have to intervene and have them spared, even though David had not spared the Amalekites children and wives? This further proves that God did not cause this, but instead tried to redeem it on David's behalf by intervening so that the children and wives were not killed. Also, if God was behind this tragedy, it would have been inconsistent for Him to allow David to recover all that the Amalekites had taken. David would not have prevailed nor recovered if it was God's will for this to happen to him. Thank You, Jesus. God, You are a good God!

Another question to ask is, "Why was the city burned?" Or, "Why didn't God prevent it from being burned?" David was not in God's perfect will at the moment this happened and God cannot bring complete protection when someone is outside of His perfect will. God works and moves in our lives to the degree that we let Him and cooperate with Him.

Mercy Killing and Assisted Suicide

So I stood upon him, and slew him, because I was sure that he could not live after that he was fallen: and I took the crown that was upon his head, and the bracelet that was on his arm, and have brought them hither unto my lord.

— 2 Samuel 1:10

And David said unto him, How wast thou not afraid to stretch forth thine hand to destroy the LORD's anointed? And David called one of the young men, and said, go near, and fall upon him. And he smote him that he died.

— 2 Samuel 1:14-15

In 1 Samuel 31, Saul asked his armor bearer to kill him (mercy kill) but when he refused to do so, Saul fell on his own sword (Suicide). This Amalekite's account was different from that account. I believe there are three explanations for that; One, Saul was possibly still alive but dying slowly when this Amalekite found him and therefore asked him to "finish him off," which he did. Two, it is possible that this man made up this story when he found Saul already dead. He then took Saul's crown and bracelet to David in order to gain his favor. Three, both scenarios could have happened. He "finished off" or mercy killed Saul at his request, then took these tidings with his crown and bracelet to David in hope for a reward or favor (2 Samuel 4:10). Nonetheless, his confession to killing Saul regardless of the reason and motive sealed his fate. David was not thrilled at the killing of Saul (2 Samuel 1:14-15).

This may be shocking to many and may also sound controversial, but I won't let that stop me from sharing what I believe is the truth! Many people believe or think that mercy killing and assisted suicide are okay. After all, the person is going to die anyway. They say, "Kill him and help him get out of his suffering." I disagree with that philosophy.

It's wrong to take another life in the name of mercy killing. There is no concept of mercy killing or assisted suicide in the scriptures and we see here in this verse that David was not pleased at this man's confession to killing Saul, although it was done at his own request. David took this as murder, and I believe God does, too. It is not our place to take another man's life to reduce their suffering and pain. Assisted killing, assisted suicide, and mercy killing all are ungodly and unbiblical.

We should do all we can to save life, including believing God for healing. Mercy killing is not the only option to free a person from pain. We should not take the easy way out.

Always Do the Right Thing

Then David took hold on his clothes, and rent them; and likewise all the men that were with him: And they mourned, and wept, and fasted until even, for Saul, and for Jonathan his son, and for the people of the LORD, and for the house of Israel; because they were fallen by the sword.

— 2 Samuel 1:11-12

We cannot take another person's actions as an excuse to not do what is right. We must be devoted to doing what is right, regardless of other people's actions.

Seeing how David had treated Saul earlier, his actions were consistent. He continuously treated him with love and respect. I do not believe for one second that he was faking it. This was a heart-driven sincere action by David (2 Samuel 1:11-12).

What would you have done if you found out that your enemy had died? Most people would throw an overnight party to celebrate the death of their enemy, but not David. David had seen the defeat of his nation, the death of his best friend Jonathan, and the death of the Lord's anointed, Saul. David did not rejoice, but he instead mourned for them all. His men also followed his leadership and mourned for the death of all the slain children of Israel, including the king and his son, Jonathan.

This is not an easy thing to do, but it is the right thing. Saul had made David a vagabond. He had pursued to kill David multiple times, but David had spared Saul's life whenever he had opportunity to kill him. Yet when his enemy, Saul, died, he mourned for him and fasted.

And they mourned, and wept, and fasted until even, for Saul, and for Jonathan his son, and for the people of the LORD, and for the house of Israel; because they were fallen by the sword.

— 2 Samuel 1:11-12

Notice the order in which this is stated. It says he mourned and fasted "for Saul, and for Jonathan his son, and for the people of the Lord, and for the house of Israel." This doesn't say he mourned for Jonathan his friend and the children of Israel. It puts Saul first, making a point of priority, and saying he was not just mourning his friend Jonathan, but also for the very man that continually sought to take his life.

But David did not stop, he went on to kill the very messenger that had "mercy-killed Saul." Why did David think this way when it was clear that Saul was his enemy? David was a godly man. He was not pleased with the death of Saul, and he punished the man who confessed to doing so. David still did not stop there.

We don't see him ever celebrating the arrival of his kingdom as a result of the death of Saul. David had every right to do so—Saul was his adversary. But he did not. If David was out to please the people like Saul was known to do, most of the people would have sided with David. They would not have been offended if he had celebrated the death of Saul, the man that had sought day and night for his life. But again, David did not view things like the world did. He was a godly man and his view was a godly view.

An average person would have asked, "What's wrong with David? Celebrate and rejoice; your enemy has died and your kingdom has also arrived." David would not buy into that thinking and would have asked, "What is wrong with you?"

Rejoice with them that do rejoice, and weep with them that weep.

— Romans 12:15

David's actions after the death of Saul clearly set him apart as a true man of God. He mourned with those who mourned, fasted with those who fasted, and wept with all who wept.

It Takes Time. Be Patient.
Wait For Your "Throne"

And it came to pass after this, that David inquired of the LORD, saying, Shall I go up into any of the cities of Judah? And the LORD said unto him, Go up. And David said, whither shall I go up? And he said, Unto Hebron.

— 2 Samuel 2:1

And the men of Judah came, and there they anointed David king over the house of Judah.

— 2 Samuel 2:4

One of the wrong perceptions people have is that God is in the sprint business. I really believe that God is in the marathon business. This can help explain why the things of God usually take time to come to fruition. When God calls someone, or anoints someone for ministry or any position, it doesn't always happen right away.

Personally, I remember when I was called to ministry. The Lord told me to go Bible school and prepare for my ministry. When dealing with God, time is involved. I don't think it is because God wants us to suffer, but because He is doing a great work of perfecting our character, attitude, wisdom, experience, and patience that will be vital for the ministry He has called us to.

David had shown tremendous, overwhelming patience to become king. David did not make this come to pass through his own strength, which I believe was a temptation he faced. He neither kicked down doors nor forced his way to the throne to become king, but instead waited for the Lord to do it for him. But even then, he did not obtain the kingdom all at once (Deuteronomy 7:22), but little by little. Just like the children of Israel did not take the land all at once, God gave it to them little by little.

Most scholars estimate David to have been about seventeen-years-old when he was first initially anointed king over Israel by Samuel in 1 Samuel 16. 2 Samuel 5:4 says that he was thirty-years-old when he began to reign over Judah, which would mean that he waited about thirteen years to begin his reign. Even then, he did not yet reign over all of Israel, but only over his tribe of Judah. It also took another seven-and-a-half years of reigning over Judah before he reigned over all of Israel from Jerusalem.

So, in total, it took about twenty years for David to see the call of God on his life as King over Israel come to fruition. David took twenty years preparing, or being prepared, for a forty-year reign as king over Israel. We must prepare and we must be patient. Very few people have an idea or concept that some things happen gradually or in phases and steps. It's like they want everything to come to fruition yesterday. Look at David: even though it took up to twenty years to be fulfilled, it happened.

However, the scriptures teach that there are steps and stages of how God moves and manifests Himself in our lives. First the blade, then the ear, then the full corn in the ear (Mark 4:28). Isaiah 28:10...13 says *"For precept must be upon precept, precept upon precept; line upon line, line upon line; here a little, and there a little: But the word of the LORD was unto them precept upon precept, precept upon precept; line upon line, line upon line; here a little, and there a little."*

Some people think that if God has said something, there would be no process, no opposition, and that it would come to pass right to its completion. We learn that since God works through people on many occasions, and these people have free will, they have to choose to cooperate with Him. Many times, God is delayed, and even hindered, by people's lack of cooperation.

There are many factors that can hinder or affect God's will from happening faster or from unfolding at all. One of those factors can be ourselves. For example, sometimes when someone is prayed for, he may not receive a full manifestation instantaneously. He may experience a gradual process, and therefore, depending on different factors and unknown circumstances, it may take some time.

It took about twenty years for David to fully become king over Israel, and it happened little by little, in steps and stages, but this man did not quit. He was patient through the entire journey. He had to persevere and fight off all the challenges that came his way, and he did not settle for a partial manifestation (King over Judah) because God called, chose, and anointed him to be king over all Israel.

What's also interesting about David is that when the opportunity came for him to be king over Judah first, he did not turn it down because he wanted to be king over Israel. **He took this as a stepping stone for him becoming king over all**

Israel. He went and sought the Lord for direction and then he made a decision on how to proceed: he did not jump on it before seeking the Lord.

Joab's Actions: Anything We Permit Will Only Increase

When Joab and all the host that was with him were come, they told Joab, saying, Abner the son of Ner came to the king, and he hath sent him away, and he is gone in peace. Then Joab came to the king, and said, what hast thou done? Behold, Abner came unto thee; why is it that thou hast sent him away, and he is quite gone? Thou knowest Abner the son of Ner, that he came to deceive thee, and to know thy going out and thy coming in, and to know all that thou doest. And when Joab was come out from David, he sent messengers after Abner, which brought him again from the well of Sirah: but David knew it not. And when Abner was returned to He-bron, Joab took him aside in the gate to speak with him quietly, and smote him there under the fifth rib, that he died, for the blood of Asahel his brother.

— 2 Samuel 3:23-27

Joab was the head of David's army while Abner was the head of Saul's and Ishbosheth's army (1 Samuel 15:50). These two were enemies because Abner had killed Asahel, Joab's brother (2 Samuel 2:22-23), though it was in self-defense. When Joab learned of Abner's visit to David, he knew his position as army commander was threatened by the same man who had killed his brother. Joab also wanted to take revenge against Abner for killing his brother, Asahel.

Joab questioned David about the visit of Abner, but it was not his place to question David as his king. Joab crossed his boundary here and David should have dealt with this behavior, but he didn't. Joab went on to send his men after Abner, who then brought him back so that he could kill him. This was all without David's approval. Again, David should have confronted this behavior.

However, David knew about the hatred between the two and did little to restrain Joab. Joab had not honored David by going after Abner and eventually killing him without his knowledge, let alone permission. David knew that Joab would want to kill Abner because he had killed his brother, Asahel. Because David did not confront and deal with this behavior of Joab, he would later regret it as this same unrestrained guy came back to defy and bite him.

Absalom had rebelled against his father, David, and committed treason. He publicly had sex with David's concubines (2 Samuel 16:21-22). He had pursued after David to kill him and when he failed, he was found alive hanging on a tree during the battle between his men and David's men. Joab went on to kill him, defying the king's orders not to do such a thing (2 Samuel 18:5,14). Joab was a liability to the godly success of David's reign, and David should have dealt with this man early on. At this point, it was more difficult to deal with him because Joab seemed indispensable. He had gained so much power and influence that he had become untouchable.

In 1 Kings 1:7, we see that Joab formed an alliance with Adonijah, David's son, who was against David and Solomon. David later instructed Solomon to have Joab killed (1 Kings 2:5; 20:30-34).

Anything we permit will only increase. David permitted this behavior of Joab to escalate, which later brought him tremendous trouble. Even when he found out about the death of Abner, he did little to punish Joab. The curse he spoke over Joab was not sufficient. David should have fired, replaced, demoted, or reduced the influence of Joab. David's lack of action promoted the bad behavior of Joab. It should not have mattered if he was family; some kind of disciplinary action was necessary.

This same man also played a part in the killing of Uriah. If only he had dismissed him earlier, David probably would have had another godly man installed in that position that would have rejected David's plea to kill Uriah. The grief that later followed David through Joab occurred because he never acted when he should have. Joab was an army general for David with much trouble.

Again, anything permitted will only increase. When we see signs of bad behavior, we should do something about it, or else we will pay the heaviest price down the road.

Put Aside Personal Issues to Honor the Positive Attributes of Another

And David said to Joab, and to all the people that were with him, Rend your clothes, and gird you with sackcloth, and mourn before Abner. And king David himself followed the bier. And they buried Abner in Hebron: and the king lifted up his voice, and wept at the grave of Abner; and all the people wept.

— 2 Samuel 3:31-32

Abner, as the army commander of Saul, sought to kill David, and spear-headed the hunt for David's life at the instruction of Saul on multiple occasions. David knew this, but when Abner died, there was no rejoicing or celebrating in David's camp, but instead mourning and fasting.

David put aside his personal issues and honored Abner and his authority as an army commander, who had fought hundreds of battles to destroy the enemies of Israel. This was a good thing. Although Abner had done some evil things, he also did some good things for the nation of Israel. Having fought all those enemies, he surely deserved to be honored and respected. As a godly leader, David got this right. He mourned and fasted for Abner and commanded his men to do the same. David chose to focus on the positives in Abner's life, not the negatives or his own personal issues.

David had respect for the authority and office of Abner. David's actions clearly sent a message to all Israel that he had nothing to do with this murder of Abner by Joab.

Capital Punishment

For when they came into the house, he lay on his bed in his bedchamber, and they smote him, and slew him, and beheaded him, and took his head, and got them away through the plain all night. And they brought the head of Ish-bosheth unto David to Hebron, and said to the king, Behold the head of Ish-bosheth the son of Saul thine enemy, which sought thy life; and the LORD hath avenged my lord the king this day of Saul, and of his seed. And David answered Rechab and Baanah his brother, the sons of Rimmon the Beerothite, and said unto them, As the LORD liveth, who hath redeemed my soul out of all adversity, When one told me, saying, Behold, Saul is dead, thinking to have brought good tidings, I took hold of him, and slew him in Ziklag, who thought that I would have given him a reward for his tidings: How much more, when wicked men have slain a righteous person in his own house upon his bed? Shall I not therefore now require his blood of your hand, and take you away from the earth? And David commanded his young men, and they slew them, and cut off their hands and their feet, and hanged them up over the pool in Hebron. But they took the head of Ish-bosheth, and buried it in the sepulcher of Abner in Hebron.

— 2 Samuel 4:7-12

It is well established that Ishbosheth (the son of King Saul) was an enemy of David, even though David was not his enemy. Ishbosheth was the son of King Saul who had survived death and was now the king over Israel while David was King of Judah. Ishbosheth had two captains, Baanah and Rechab, who one day went to his house and killed him while he was sleeping on his bed.

This was not war. It was not self-defense, but murder. These two men connived and murdered a man who was innocent and took his head to King David, thinking David would rejoice and give them reward for what they did. To their surprise, David's response was very different from their expectations. These men had killed their king (boss). This was wrong and David knew it. David said that they were wicked men who had slain a righteous person in his own house upon his bed (2 Samuel 4:11). These men took matters into their own hands killing their own boss, king Ishbosheth. David was not going to let them off the hook for this murder. David had them receive a capital punishment for the murder they had committed against Ishbosheth, the king of Israel.

Some people are against capital punishment, but it is a godly form of justice when it is administered by authority against one who is found guilty of murder. There is a place for capital punishment, and here we see a good example of it. These two men were killed for murdering another man. They were not given life in prison or a few years in prison. David executed them on behalf of Ishbosheth.

This also teaches that capital punishment is not wrong. Many people today are against, but not God. He that takes a life of another should pay with his own life. Of course, there are exceptions to this, such as righteous war, self-defense or defending the innocent. David laid a precedent that capital punishment is a godly thing. David was a true, godly leader. He did not rejoice over the death of Ishbosheth, but mourned and executed judgment on his behalf.

We see a similar action when a man came from war and told David that he had mercy-killed Saul upon his request (2 Samuel 1:1-16). This man came to David to give him the "good" tidings of Saul's death, thinking that he would have been pleased by the news. But, David killed this man for killing Saul (2 Samuel 4:10).

It Will Finally Come To Pass. Here Comes the King, Behold David the King of Israel

So all the elders of Israel came to the king to Hebron; and king David made a league with them in Hebron before the LORD: and they anointed David king over Israel.

— 2 Samuel 5:3

If we do not give up, if we do not quit, we will finally win. David is a wonderful example of that statement. It looked like his ascendance to the throne would never come. It seemed so distant, while the temptation to compromise was continuous. It may also have seemed that he would never be king over Israel, but only Judah. It indeed took time, approximately twenty years to become king over Israel, but it did come to pass. It happened not through David's own strength, but through God.

Patience and dependency on God is one of the most important characteristics that helped get the arrival of his kingdom across the finish line. We also learn that God will work to fulfill what He has spoken (Habakkuk 2:2-3) and sometimes it might happen in steps and stages. We have to learn this patience game. It is the key to winning, to becoming a humble person, to walking in God's kind of love, to promotion, and to building good character. Patience is a very vital aspect of a man's character. May the Lord develop and help you manifest this fruit of patience.

Do Not Be a Man Pleaser

And David said unto Michal, It was before the LORD, which chose me before thy father, and before all his house, to appoint me ruler over the people of the LORD, over Israel: therefore will I play before the LORD.

— 2 Samuel 6:21

David was the very opposite of King Saul in every way. He always sought to do things that were pleasing to God or unto the Lord, not unto man. In 2 Samuel 6, he had a desire to bring the Ark of the Covenant back to the city of David. David danced unto the Lord with all his might as the ark was in the city of David. There was rejoicing and shouting in the city that had been deprived of the Ark of the Covenant for years. But as he did, his wife Michal, Saul's daughter, despised him. She thought that David was dancing unto men, yet it was all unto the Lord. Unlike Saul, David did not care what people thought (including his wife, Michal) about him dancing unto the Lord, as long as He (God) was blessed by his actions.

This is the same attitude we should always exhibit. We should be seekers to please God, not men. We can learn this lesson from David. He was a king, a very dignified position, and he didn't have to dance, which could lead to being despised by the people. But David was not dancing for the people, but for the Lord. There was a difference, and therefore he didn't care at all what the people thought of him, but what God thought of him, the One Whom had chosen him king over Israel (2 Samuel 6:21-22). David would have done it all the same all over again because it was unto the Lord. There is no need for shame when we are doing things unto the Lord and not unto men.

Those who do not love the Lord despise and criticize those who are praising the Lord. The example here is Michal (2 Samuel 6:20). And in the Gospels, we see the example of Mary (Matthew 26:7; Mark 14:3; Luke 7:37-38; John 12:3). Those who love the Lord would do anything, even if it would result in self-debasing, as long as it pleased the Lord. Satan will always parade someone to despise and criticize you regardless of what you do. We should always maintain and stick to our convictions and not be ashamed.

Colossians 3:23-24 says *"And whatsoever ye do, do it heartily, as to the Lord, and not unto men; knowing that of the Lord ye shall receive the reward of the inheritance; for ye serve the Lord Christ."*

Patriot

And David perceived that the LORD had established him king over Israel, and that he had exalted his kingdom for his people Israel's sake.

— 2 Samuel 5:12

One of the most outstanding characteristics of David was that he loved his people and country. He loved God, which was the main reason he loved Israel—God's chosen people. We see this through his actions. I believe that if David never loved Israel, he would not have been chosen. God wanted a man that would lead, protect, and defend the people of Israel while putting Him first.

David went hard after the enemies of Israel—the Philistines, Moabites, Syrians, Amalekites, and Ammonites (2 Samuel 8)—because he loved Israel. David fought Goliath, who came against the people of Israel. He fought Philistines who defied the children of Israel. Most people who have a love for country also tend to have a fear of the Lord. David loved Israel by loving the Lord.

This explains why some people join the military and desire to serve their country. We learn from the life of David that it's a godly thing to love our country. David was a patriot. It's ungodly not to love your country. Godly people love their country and the people in it.

Doing The Right Thing But Not Following The Given Procedure and Instructions

And they set the ark of God upon a new cart, and brought it out of the house of Abinadab that was in Gibeah: and Uzzah and Ahio, the sons of Abinadab, drove the new cart.

— 2 Samuel 6:3

Here is a lesson that very few people pay attention to. Here we see that David wanted to move the Ark of the Covenant from the house of Abinadab to the city of David. This was a good thing, and I believe God was delighted because King Saul never even had a single thought of doing this. However, the good and right thing was done in a wrong way. The right instructions and procedures were not followed. There were prescribed ways and order to follow when moving and transporting the ark, but these men did not follow the prescribed order. We can't just hide behind good intentions, but we must follow the prescribed order and rules. Ignorance of the law and directions of how to transport the Ark of the Covenant was no excuse. See Numbers 4:15 and Exodus 25:15.

We must do the right things, following the right and prescribed order. Many times, people do not want to follow the prescribed order of doing things as long as they do the right thing. This is a wrong attitude. Although the actions are commendable and admirable, we must strive to do both the right thing and also follow the prescribed order of doing those things. If only the right order was followed while transporting the ark, this man's life (Uzzah) would not have been lost (2 Samuel 6:7). David and these men should have known better (Numbers 4:15). It was not God's fault because He was just following through with His commands and instructions of how the ark was to be treated and transported. **Doing the right thing is not enough; we must follow the prescribed order and instructions (2 Samuel 6:3).**

David violated God's instructions and his man paid a heavy price with his own life. This was David's fault (Numbers 3:31, Deuteronomy 10:8). Good intentions were not enough. These good intentions did not save this man's life. If David had followed the instructions and procedure, the story would have been different. The ark is similar to God's Word, or say that it contained God's Word. It can release life and blessing or release curses depending on your response.

Later, when David adjusted and did the right thing and followed the instructions given by God in His Word, no man was killed, meaning it was done correctly the second time. We should always seek to do things God's way. If we are doing a God thing or a good thing, it must always be done God's way, following the given instructions, or else we miss out on and hinder the flow of God's blessing in our lives.

Does the Married Woman In This Situation Get A Pass?

And David sent messengers, and took her; and she came in unto him, and he lay with her; for she was purified from her uncleanness: and she returned unto her house.

— 2 Samuel 11:4

I know this section could rub some people the wrong way, but please hear my heart. I'm not saying Bathsheba is all to blame, but I'm presenting a few thoughts that I have had and a viewpoint that I believe that many people have never given detailed thought. The guilt of King David is apparent to everyone, but I believe that the part played by Bathsheba in this sexual affair is often overlooked.

Could Bathsheba have played a major part in this sin? Did she do anything wrong to fan the flames of this behavior? Were all women bathing out in the open as Bathsheba did? I strongly doubt it. Was she out to entice the king or any man? I personally would not entirely dismiss it, mainly because we see how ungodly society is today and the Bible says that nothing is new in the earth. What people are doing today has been done in the past.

Even so, the greatest responsibility rested on David's shoulders. He knew better. He was a leader. He had to be an example to the people he was appointed king.

It looks so simple and easy, even though Bathsheba was being called by the king. It just seems to me like she was anticipating the call. This makes me think that Bathsheba played a big part in this adultery. I also believe she was not forced to go to the king. There is no proof of compulsion in this, even though it was the king who had called. This offer from the king was so good, she couldn't turn it down. She wouldn't reject it. "Forget my husband! The king is in need of my services," she probably thought.

Again, there was no resistance on her part. Zero resistance, no back and forth, but a seamlessly easy answer to the king's request. Why is this? I'm also not convinced that it was because she was afraid of the king and therefore had to do as he said. I do not buy the thinking that David would have killed her had she not responded positively, but even if he did, it would have been the right thing for her to do to reject the king. That would have been a noble and godly death instead of giving in to this ungodly demand.

She was a married woman and had every right to say no to this king who had more than enough wives. I do not believe that David would have gone to the extreme of killing her, had she rejected him. What sort of woman was this? Was she a low-life? Was she in heat like David? Was she in for the money and reputation of being the king's wife?

Bathsheba could have refused any advancements from the king first by not bathing out in the open, knowing what that would have led to. But also, she could have replied to the king noting that she was married. No matter how you want to look at this, it was an adulterous affair on both parties part. This was no rape. She was willing.

If David was so much in heat, it would have been ethical for her as a married woman to risk being beaten or threatened rather than to just lay down without any hesitation. Does that show that she enabled and cooperated with the king in this adulterous affair? After all, her husband had been gone to war and the king had her back covered the whole way. This woman was another guilty adulterer just like King David, and she clearly enabled this adultery. I really believe this.

Also, let me ask, did she ever let her husband Uriah know of what had happened? Did she let him know what the king had done, assuming she did it out of threat? Why not? Why didn't she? I see a lot of cover-up on her part. Bathsheba concealed and covered up this sin like David did. Was she really a wife or a harlot? It took two people to commit this sin. Both Bathsheba and King David were guilty. No excuses.

Another interesting thing is that David did not send soldiers to her. He sent "messengers," meaning this could not have been forceful. It strongly appears to me that she got exactly what she was looking for. This is a classic example that shows that it takes two people to cooperate with this kind of sin. However, more was expected of David, and therefore he receives the bigger blame. She was responsible, but King David was more responsible.

Here are a few things we can take away from this episode between David and Bathsheba:

I) David was in the wrong place at the wrong time. This was a time kings go to battle, not to bed! He should have been at war, not in Jerusalem (2 Samuel 11:1). Had he been doing what God anointed Him to do, this would not have happened.

II) What are you doing with a married man or woman? Our society today has no reverence for marriage. If David and Bathsheba respected the covenant that each had with their spouses, they wouldn't have gone down this road. Hebrews 13:4 says *"Marriage is honorable in all, and the bed undefiled: but whoremongers and adulterers God will judge."* Any advances, requests made against a married person, are straight out wrong. No discussion!

III) David was in a similar situation as Joseph was (Genesis 39:7-9), but Joseph did not go towards a compromising situation, but fled from it (Sexual affair with a married woman). Like Joseph, we should flee any appearance of evil (1 Thessalonians 5:22).

IV) When we are dealing with an issue, we should always examine both sides to the problem (Proverbs 18:13) to prevent it from happening again. Focusing only on one side will probably enable it to be repeated. Lastly, we should always seek to choose to do what is right. We will continually be presented with ungodly opportunities, but it's up to us to choose what is godly.

A Man After God's Own Heart

But now thy kingdom shall not continue: the LORD hath sought him a man after his own heart, and the LORD hath commanded him to be captain over his people, because thou hast not kept that which the LORD commanded thee.

— 1 Samuel 13:14

Although David's behavior was extremely detestable, this did not change the fact that David was still a man after God's own heart. His behavior was not depicting that he was truly a man after God's own heart, but God did not call him a man after His own heart because of his wonderful, perfect behavior. If that was so, then God would have referred to him as such after he grossly sinned in the situation with Bathsheba. So, we know that David being called a man after God's own heart was not because he was a perfect or sinless man. David had some flaws, but he also sought to get right with God on a regular basis, even after he had fallen. He was a man who always sought to please God, not man.

In the same way, we are not God's children because we

are sinless or perfect. Nothing is further from the truth. It is not our performance that qualifies us, but our relationship with God through faith in Jesus. If our sinlessness were the reason for anything good in our lives, none of us would ever qualify. It's astounding to see that David got his heart hardened to the Lord, but this did not happen overnight. David was slowly and gradually departing from seeking the Lord for him to commit adultery and murder.

Remember Your Friends and Keep Your Word

And David said, Is there yet any that is left of the house of Saul, that I may show him kindness for Jonathan's sake?

— 2 Samuel 9:1

David was quite a unique guy. He could have forgotten about Jonathan, but he didn't. It took a long time for David to remember this covenant, but he ultimately remembered. David had made a covenant with Jonathan to show him kindness and not to cut off kindness from his house forever (1 Samuel: 13-17). David followed through with his word. He demonstrated integrity by doing exactly as he said.

Jonathan had a son named Mephibosheth who fell and broke his legs and became lame as his nurse fled after hearing of the death of Saul and Jonathan. David reached out to him to show him kindness for Jonathan's sake. David was honoring Jonathan by honoring his son Mephibosheth. It was all for Jonathan (2 Samuel 9:7). We should never forget those that have been good to us and those to whom we have given our word. Jonathan had been a true good friend to David, and had it not been for Jonathan, David would not be alive.

David was not self-focused or self-centered. He did not have to remember his covenant with Jonathan—after all he was long gone. No one would have known that he hadn't kept his word, but he still went out to keep it. He did not have to remember Mephibosheth, yet he did, and in a big way.

The way David treated Mephibosheth is very symbolic of how the Lord has treated us and displays what He has done for us:

I) Mephibosheth did not deserve to live, but to die. He had done nothing to deserve to live, but neither did we. We were all deserving to die and go to hell, but Jesus changed our story.

II) David remembered the covenant he made with Jonathan the same way God remembered the covenant He made with Jesus. Because of this covenant, God had mercy on us. Just as Mephibosheth benefited from a covenant that was not made with him, we all benefited from a covenant that was not made with us.

III) David extended undeserved favor, kindness, and mercy to Mephibosheth, and God did the same for us. There is nothing we receive from God because of, or based on, our goodness. It's all by God's grace, mercy, kindness, and favor. Thank You, Jesus, for Your favor upon our lives. Mephibosheth dined with the king continually, and we also get to dine with King Jesus continually. Mephibosheth got what he did not deserve instead of what he deserved.

IV) Gracious invitation to the great King. What Mephibosheth experienced through King David is exactly what we experienced through King Jesus. He was invited by the King, David, just as we were invited by Jesus—the King of kings. He received all this good treatment because of Jonathan, for Jonathan's sake, or in the name of Jonathan. We also receive all the blessings and favor from God for Jesus' sake, or in the name of Jesus. It's all about Jesus—not us—and it was all about Jonathan—not Mephibosheth—although he was the beneficiary. It did not stop there; Mephibosheth received all that pertained to Saul and to his entire household. A man who was lame and poor became rich and blessed. We were also once poor, but when we allowed Jesus into our hearts, we received all things that pertain to the kingdom of God (2 Peter 1:3). Thank You, Jesus!

A stranger became a son (2 Samuel 9:11). Mephibosheth was elevated to the status of a king's son. What a blessing this was to this man! In the same way, we were once strangers, but when Jesus came in, we were elevated to become children of God (John 1:13; Galatians 3:26; Romans 8:14-17). Thank You, Jesus for making us God's children.

Busy Doing Nothing!

And it came to pass, after the year was expired, at the time when kings go forth to battle, that David sent Joab, and his servants with him, and all Israel; and they destroyed the children of Ammon, and besieged Rabbah. But David tarried still at Jerusalem. And it came to pass in an eveningtide, that David arose from off his bed, and walked upon the roof of the king's house: and from the roof he saw a woman washing herself; and the woman was very beautiful to look upon.

— 2 Samuel 11:1-2

As the old saying goes, that an idle mind is the devil's workshop. Being idle is one of the ways the enemy can begin to have an inroad in our lives. David, who was anointed king, was in the wrong place at the wrong time. He was home sleeping all day long and got up in the evening. The morning was a time when kings went to battle, not to bed. This was very wrong for David, who was anointed to lead Israel, to be home and not at battle. David was leading from behind and the enemy struck.

David had experienced success and I believe he started slowing down on seeking the Lord. The enemy took advantage of him becoming sluggish and not industrious, as he ought to have been. If you have time for sin, you will sin.

David had some serious sexual problems, but all these were self-inflicted because he had broken God's command against multiplying wives (Deuteronomy 17:15-17). David had lots of wives already (2 Samuel 3:2-5; 2 Samuel 5:13) at this point, but was still not satisfied. This was typical lust. If six or seven wives won't make you satisfied, one more won't. If David had not gone against God's original command of Deuteronomy 17:15-17, he would not have had this problem. He cracked the door open and the enemy squeezed through and started to destroy his life.

We must not give the devil access by being idle. We must be occupied and busy doing what God has called us to do. Be active, following God's instructions and directions. We are to occupy until He comes and redeems the time as well.

She Is Married – Get Your Hands Off of Her

And David sent and inquired after the woman. And one said, Is not this Bath-sheba, the daughter of Eliam, the wife of Uriah the Hittite?

— 2 Samuel 11:3

What a big mistake trying to talk to a married woman. What was David trying to do inquiring after the married woman? Something was terribly wrong with him. He had slipped from seeking the Lord wholeheartedly, or else this would not have happened. David had zero respect for this woman, Bathsheba, as we can see his advances even when it was clearly spelt out that she was married. He also had no respect for her husband, Uriah, who was a great soldier fighting faithfully for his country and king. David was like a horse that had no understanding.

Be ye not as the horse, or as the mule, which have no understanding: whose mouth must be held in with bit and bridle, lest they come near unto thee.

— Psalm 32:9

But whoso committeth adultery with a woman lack-eth understanding: he that doeth it destroyeth his own soul.

— Proverbs 6:32

He was like a "bull" in heat that wanted to help himself out. This was not a "love affair." David used this woman and then sent her home. What a shame! This was unacceptable.

Can a man take fire in his bosom, and his clothes not be burned? Can one go upon hot coals, and his feet not be burned? So he that goeth in to his neighbour's wife; whosoever toucheth her shall not be innocent. Men do not despise a thief, if he steal to satisfy his soul when he is hungry; But if he be found, he shall restore sevenfold; he shall give all the substance of his house.

— Proverbs 6:27-31

David played with fire in his bosom and he got burned. He was not innocent for having relations with his neighbor's wife. He was a thief who stole to satisfy his lustful soul, and when he got caught by God through Nathan, he was re-paid with interest, and his house was plagued with trouble. David was very self-centered, and he wasn't seeking and actively following the Lord. What had come over this man? He was such a terrific example in his early life, but now he began to slip into things that we probably would never have imagined.

He was waking up at a time he was supposed to be going to bed (evening-tide). David's brain was shot. He was thinking with his lustful emotions. The fact that Bathsheba was a married woman should have been a red flag for David. This should have been a red flag for anyone, but especially David who was known for seeking after the Lord. This was a steep descent on David's part. David was told that this was a married woman, but he was so disconnected that he either ignored this warning or he was so dull.

It's a very simple lesson that we should not miss. We should stay miles away from a married man or woman. Why would one want to be the vessel that the devil uses to wreck and destroy another person's marriage? If someone is married, that alone should be a red flag. Period.

David's heart was hardened. He wasn't actively seeking the Lord, as we see by his actions of being in bed instead of leading war. We must set boundaries to protect ourselves from falling. We should stay in our lane.

David had no shame. What had happened to his conscience? This behavior of David goes back to him having ungodly sexual relationships by having many wives and concubines (2 Samuel 5:13 and 2 Samuel 3:2-5).

Solomon could have learned about being a womanizer from his father. After all, the apple does not usually fall far from the tree. Sometimes, kids learn more by vision than by confession.

I pray that God will give you wisdom to make wise, sane, and godly decisions. May you use your heart and your brain, and not your emotions, in making decisions. May God give you a revelation between love and lust. Resist the devil and he shall flee from you.

The Cover Up

And the woman conceived, and sent and told David, and said, I am with child. And David sent to Joab, saying, Send me Uriah the Hittite. And Joab sent Uriah to David. And when Uriah was come unto him, David demanded of him how Joab did, and how the people did, and how the war prospered. And David said to Uriah, Go down to thy house, and wash thy feet. And Uriah departed out of the king's house, and there followed him a mess of meat from the king. But Uriah slept at the door of the king's house with all the servants of his lord, and went not down to his house. And when they had told David, saying, Uriah went not down unto his house, David said unto Uriah, Camest thou not from thy journey? Why then didst thou not go down unto thine house? And Uriah said unto David, The ark, and Israel, and Judah, abide in tents; and my lord Joab, and the servants of my lord, are encamped in the open fields; shall I then go into mine house, to eat and to drink, and to lie with my wife? as thou livest, and as thy soul liveth, I will not do this thing. And David said to Uriah, Tarry here today also, and tomorrow I will let thee depart. So Uriah abode in Jerusalem that day, and the morrow. And when David had called him, he did eat and drink before him; and he made him drunk: and at even he went out to lie on his bed with the servants of his lord, but went not down to his house.

—2 Samuel 11:5-13

David was now in trouble. Bathsheba was pregnant and now he began to seek to cover up this adultery and pregnancy. Although Bathsheba played a part in this sin as an enabler and a concealer of the truth from her husband Uriah, David personally took the concealment to another level.

David should have repented at this point. Quick repentance could have led him not to kill Uriah. But David was so hardened unto the Lord that he was not willing to repent, at least not quite yet. David was not seeking the Lord.

He tried his best to use his position and authority to cover his tracks. He began to use Uriah in an effort to cover up his mess. He sent him home after getting him drunk, hoping that he would go home and sleep with his wife, thereby concealing the pregnancy. This was typical hypocrisy on David's part. David did not stop there!

When he saw that sending Uriah home in an effort to sleep with his wife did not work, he moved on with a plan to get him killed. This was such a sorry situation in that David disrespected Uriah so much that he used him to try to cover his tracks by sleeping with his wife. When that failed, he had him carry a note that contained his death sentence, and because of Uriah's integrity and respect for the king, he did not open it.

In the same way, David used Bathsheba and never loved her. This was no love affair, but a lust affair. David was behaving like the devil. This behavior was very detestable. David had no jealousy for Bathsheba that he was willing to have Uriah have sexual intercourse with her. Did he really love her? What kind of man would be willing to let another man sleep with a woman he loves? There would have been some sort of jealousy. How fallen and gone from the Lord had David become?

When we sin, it is wiser and better to repent there and then. If we procrastinate, we will end up covering up that sin with another sin, and then another, which will eventually make it even harder to stop. The quicker we repent, the lesser need for a cover-up. It shouldn't have taken David over nine months to repent (2 Samuel 12:13-14).

He that covereth his sins shall not prosper: but whoso confesseth and forsaketh them shall have mercy.

— Proverbs 28:13

David's Downward Spiral

And it came to pass, after the year was expired, at the time when kings go forth to battle, that David sent Joab, and his servants with him, and all Israel; and they destroyed the children of Ammon, and besieged Rabbah. But David tarried still at Jerusalem. And it came to pass in an eveningtide, that David arose from off his bed, and walked upon the roof of the king's house: and from the roof he saw a woman washing herself; and the woman was very beautiful to look upon. And David sent and inquired after the woman. And one said, Is not this Bath-sheba, the daughter of Eliam, the wife of Uriah the Hittite? And David sent messengers, and took her; and she came in unto him, and he lay with her; for she was purified from her uncleanness: and she returned unto her house. And the woman conceived, and sent and told David, and said, I am with child. And David sent to Joab, saying, Send me Uriah the Hittite. And Joab sent Uriah to David. And when Uriah was come unto him, David demanded of him how Joab did, and how the people did, and how the war prospered. And David said to Uriah, Go down to thy house, and wash thy feet. And Uriah departed out of the king's house, and there followed him a mess of meat from the king. But Uriah slept at the door of the king's house with all the servants of his lord, and went not down to his house. And when they had told David, saying, Uriah went not down unto his house, David said unto Uriah, Camest thou not from thy journey? Why then didst thou not go down unto thine house? And Uriah said unto David, The ark, and Israel, and Judah, abide in tents; and my lord Joab, and the servants of my lord, are encamped in the open fields; shall I then go into mine house, to eat and to drink, and to lie with my wife? As thou livest, and as thy soul liveth, I will not do this thing. And David said to Uriah, Tarry here today also, and tomorrow I will let thee depart. So Uriah abode in Jerusalem that day, and the morrow. And when David had called him, he did eat and *drink before him; and he made him drunk: and at even he went out to lie on his bed with the servants of his lord, but went not down to his house. And it came to pass in the morning, that David wrote a letter to Joab, and sent it by the hand of Uriah. And he wrote in the letter, saying, Set ye Uriah in the forefront of the hottest battle, and retire ye from him, that he may be smitten, and die. And it came to pass, when Joab observed the city, that he assigned Uriah unto a place where he knew that valiant men were. And the men of the city went out, and fought with Joab: and there fell some of the people of the servants of David; and Uriah the Hittite died also.*

—2 Samuel 11:1-17

David gravely sinned, but it all happened sequentially: First, He was sluggish (not seeking the Lord), then committed adultery, next lied and concealed the truth, then murdered, and lastly neglected his integrity and godly principles. At this point of David's life, there is no better way to describe him. It all starts with David multiplying wives against God's command (Deuteronomy 17:15-17). As soon as David broke that command, he was on his way to break many others. He was then sleeping all day long when he should have been at war doing exactly what God anointed him to do. David became comfortable and slothful, which led him to committing adultery with Bathsheba. He then concealed the truth from Uriah, using him for selfish reasons and finally murdering this innocent man so that he could not only cover up his sin, but have his wife for himself (2 Samuel 11:27). The Lord was not pleased with David's behavior.

There were steps in all these sins. They did not all happen instantly. David had quit seeking the Lord and was hardened against Him. His delayed repentance led him to committing sin after sin. We do not become hardened to the Lord overnight. It happens gradually as we ignore all the warning signs the Lord tries to send us. A godly man doesn't fall suddenly; it all begins when he starts to slip and he does nothing to reverse course.

There is no doubt that Uriah was a far better man and more principled than King David at this point in time. He refused to even go and have relations with his own wife knowing that his fellow soldiers were out in battle. Uriah's conscience was more acute than King David's. Even as a drunk man, he reasoned much better than David. He had more integrity than the mentally unhinged king at this time.

What had happened to David? David did not only kill Uriah, but painted a picture to try and make it look as if the man died as a war casualty. Not only that, but David grossly used the same man to deliver a note that commanded Joab to have him killed. How disconnected had David become? I can't even find the right words to depict where David was at this moment in his relationship with God. I can only say his behavior was like the devil personified. He was very cold-hearted and merciless.

How about Joab, David's general? I strongly believe that this man was just as ungodly, as we saw before when he murdered Abner. He did not even think twice or oppose the king for this evil of killing one of his soldiers, who was probably one of the best. What an insecure guy! Joab also condoned and enabled this murder. He knew better, but he partnered and connived with David in this crime. It sometimes takes more than one person to sin, either directly or indirectly. There has to be an enabler to the main sinner. Is this blind loyalty, or what? If only David had earlier fired Joab, he would not have gone this far with this sin (2 Samuel 3:12-33). Some other general would have probably stood up against this murder. We can disobey civil authority if they tell us to do anything ungodly or go against God. We can disobey yet submit to higher authorities. We are not to blindly follow ungodly commands (Acts 4:17-21).

We should always avoid surrounding ourselves with people that would enable, condone, and participate in our sins. They are the wrong people to have close to us.

And the men of the city went out, and fought with Joab: and there fell some of the people of the servants of David; and Uriah the Hittite died also.

— 2 Samuel 11:17

This verse shows clearly that other men died in the process of David wanting to kill Uriah, yet foolish Joab did nothing about it. What a sorry leader Joab was! **David not only killed Uriah, but he also killed all these soldiers that died fighting alongside Uriah.**

The Long-Suffering God

Contrary to what I have heard most people say about David being quick to repent, I don't see that in this situation with Bathsheba and Uriah. Taking over nine months to me doesn't seem like "quick to repent." However, I see how quick he was to repent in another incident he had when he numbered the children of Israel against God's direction (1 Chronicles 21:1). It's quite interesting to see that David did not repent until the child that was conceived with Bathsheba was born. How do we know this?

It says clearly that it's after the Prophet Nathan came to him and the child had been born that he repented. I wonder why God would wait nine to ten months to rebuke David? I mean it's quite interesting to see the kindness of God towards David. God is a kind God. There is hope for you and I.

God gave David opportunity and time to repent for over nine months. David could have rolled back some of the damage he had caused had he repented earlier. David was so disconnected that he was afforded a lot of time to repent, but he never acted on it until he was confronted by Nathan (2 Samuel 12:13-14). If we fail to humble ourselves, the only option is for us to be humiliated or forced to humble ourselves. Only God knows if David could have repented anytime sooner than nine months. David had lost his first love for the Lord. He was so hardened unto the Lord that he still couldn't see his sin until he got confronted. However, to his credit, he received the rebuke humbly. Most kings and people would not take it from anyone who tried to confront them and expose their sin.

David had lost his sense of discernment and judgment. If David had repented the very night he went into Bathsheba, things would not have gotten so bad. The sooner the better!

The longer we take to repent, the more our hearts become hardened to the Lord. We should be very swift to repent. No procrastinating!

It's quite encouraging to know that the Lord will give us time to repent before He officially or personally sends rebuke. That being said, it's always wiser and smarter to repent quicker because we are able to see clearly and stop the further growth of sin. David was disconnected for over nine months. Why wait so long to repent?

Despised The Commandment Of The Lord

Wherefore hast thou despised the commandment of the LORD, to do evil in his sight? thou hast killed Uriah the Hittite with the sword, and hast taken his wife to be thy wife, and hast slain him with the sword of the children of Ammon. Now therefore the sword shall never depart from thine house; because thou hast despised me, and hast taken the wife of Uriah the Hittite to be thy wife.

— 2 Samuel 12:9-10

Although David had committed multiple sins, this was not the very **root** of all these sins that David committed. David had despised the commandment of the Lord, hence doing evil in His sight. One of the main reasons we sin is because we depart from God's Word, then we begin to see things in our own understanding; we quit depending on God and seeking after Him.

David had departed from his first love. David was no longer seeking after God. He had become prosperous, rich, and there was peace in the land. He had arrived in his own eyes. The most vulnerable place to be is when we have attained what we were believing for. When we are successful, we tend to slow down on seeking the Lord, and then Satan strikes. Temptation comes with a greater wave when we are successful. We need to seek the Lord season in and season out. **We can't take a vacation or days off from seeking the Lord.**

Again, if only David had hearkened to Deuteronomy 17:15-17, he could, or would have avoided all these problems and sins he committed. A lack of hearkening to God's command opened a door the enemy eventually used to bring David down. Sinning against a brother is also sinning against God. David's sin was much more a sin against the Lord than it was against Uriah or Bathsheba. I am not saying that he did not sin against them, but in the eyes of God, it was more of a sin against Him. David sinned against God before he even sinned against Uriah and Bathsheba. Joseph put it well when he said, *"How then can I do this great wickedness, and sin against God?"* (Genesis 39:9). **If we are not afraid to sin against God, we will not be afraid to sin against any man, no matter how powerful he is. The greatest deterrent to sin should be not to sin against God.**

Joseph understood this well. This is one of the greatest motivation not to sin. David also later got this revelation. In Psalm 51:4, he says, *"Against thee, thee only, have I sinned, and done this evil in thy sight."* He understood that his sin was indeed against the Lord.

David also knew that it was wrong to mess with a married woman. You cannot take another man's wife. Even if giving David more wives was not God's perfect will (Deuteronomy 17:15-17), God would have given David more wives if that's what it took not to commit adultery with another man's wife. David was never satisfied with all the wives he had. This further shows that this was a lust problem that many wives could not fix. What a shame! **The despising of God's Word is equivalent to despising God, because God and His Word are One.**

David Reaped What He Sowed With Interest

Thus saith the LORD, Behold, I will raise up evil against thee out of thine own house, and I will take thy wives before thine eyes, and give them unto thy neighbor, and he shall lie with thy wives in the sight of this sun.

— 2 Samuel 12:11

David was not going to get away with this evil. He was going to pay the price. The Lord pronounced judgment upon him. God is not a respecter of persons (Roman 2:11) and He was not going to allow David to get away with these grievous sins that he committed. David got his share of punishment. The other way you can put it is that from the flesh he reaped what he sowed with interest. David paid for his actions, enormously. He had stolen another man's wife (2 Samuel 12:6), but the repercussions were even more devastating.

Nathan came to see David and told him a story about this rich man who had a lot of flocks and herds at his disposal, but decided to go after the one little ewe that the poor man had. The rich man killed the ewe for his guest instead of one from his lots of herds and flocks. Hypocrite David got so angry and said such a man shall surely die and restore the lamb fourfold. After David prescribed his judgment to that rich man, Nathan turned around and said, "Thou art the man."

I can only wonder what David's facial expression was as soon as he had heard that statement. I believe he turned red in the face and his heart was pounding faster than the speed of light. If only David was gracious in his judgment to the rich man, his punishment could have been lighter, but because he wasn't, he got exactly what he wished that rich man to get except death (2 Samuel 12:13-14). David was the one who was supposed to die because of his sin against Uriah and Bathsheba (2 Samuel 11) yet a pure, sinless child born out of his relationship with Bathsheba died in David's place. The child did nothing deserving of death. This child was a picture of Christ. We sinned and it's us that were supposed to die, yet Jesus, who was holy, pure, and sinless, died in our place.

Proverbs 6:27-31 says, *"Can a man take fire in his bosom, and his clothes not be burned? Can one go upon hot coals, and his feet not be burned? So, he that goeth in to his neighbour's wife; whosoever toucheth her shall not be innocent. Men do not despise a thief, if he steals to satisfy his soul when he is hungry; but if he be found, he shall restore sevenfold; he shall give all the substance of his house."*

David played with fire in his bosom and he got burned. He was not innocent for having relations with his neighbor's wife. He was a thief that stole to satisfy his lustful soul and when he got caught by God through Nathan, he restored astronomically with interest and his house was plagued with trouble.

Here we see David's troubles begin to unfold as a harvest for his sins:

I) David had his daughter Tamar raped by Amnon her half-brother. This was pure incest in addition to rape (2 Samuel 13:1-39).

II) Absalom killed his brother Amnon for raping and committing incest with his sister, Tamar (2 Samuel 13:1-39).

III) Absalom committed treason and led a civil war against David (2 Samuel 16).

IV) The child conceived in this adulterous relationship died (2 Samuel 12:13-14).

V) Absalom slept with his father's concubines publicly (2 Samuel 16:21-22 and 2 Samuel 12:12).

David brought this trouble upon himself. Looking at what the punishment was for David's actions, there is no reason why someone would want to ruin their lives and bring all this shame upon themselves in exchange for ten to twenty minutes of pleasure. This was not a smart move for David. I bet David regretted his decisions even more when the reaping kicked in. Sin is emotional. It is not smart. This is what we get when we shut off our brains just for a few minutes. What a mess David brought upon himself and his household.

David was in the Old Testament before Jesus came; his sins had not been paid for because Jesus had not died yet. His sins were imputed to him (Psalm 32:1), but for us under the new covenant, our sins have all been paid for and imputed to Jesus. We do not have to pay for our sins because Jesus made the payment already, once for all time. However, the law of sowing and reaping is still in effect. Therefore, we reap what we sow (Galatians 6:7-8). Just as there is a time for sowing, surely there is a time for reaping.

Repent and Take Responsibility For Your Actions

And David said unto Nathan, I have sinned against the LORD. And Nathan said unto David, The LORD also hath put away thy sin; thou shalt not die.

— 2 Samuel 12:13

Finally, David arose from his spiritual slumber and he repented. Although it took him almost ten months to repent, he finally did. Congratulations to David for finally realizing that he was wrong and repenting! We can only imagine what would have happened to him and his kingdom had he not repented. It takes humility for a person to humble themselves and repent.

Notice that David never pointed a single finger. He didn't say, "It was this woman who went bathing out in public. I wouldn't have sinned had she not done that. She was trying to entice me and because I'm a man, I couldn't resist it." David never gave a single excuse. He took 100% of the responsibility. What a lesson! He didn't blame anyone else, even though I can argue that Bathsheba played a major part in this grievous sexual immorality—she did not take his pants off.

David could have blamed his messengers for not advising him righteously. He could have blamed Bathsheba, Joab, and the messengers who were the enablers of his sins. All these excuses do not hold water.

One of the most common mistakes that people make is to apologize and take responsibility, but then they say, "but so and so made me do such and such or I wouldn't have done it had they not done this." This is still not taking responsibility, but rather shifting the blame. **As long as we still have any excuse or blame in our apology, we have ruined what would have been a good apology. David apologized and took full responsibility for his actions.** He said, "I have sinned against the Lord." Notice that he said "I," not Bathsheba, the messengers or Joab.

David gave no excuse. He took 100% of the responsibility without any "buts" and without sharing or shifting blame to other people, even though they could have been guilty in some way, shape, or form. A truly repentant person must take responsibility for their actions without giving any excuse or blame-shifting. If someone doesn't do it this way, then we can rest assured that they are not fully repentant. True repentance requires taking responsibility for our actions without pointing any fingers and without any "buts." Even if it clearly involved two people, we must take responsibility of our part or actions and leave the other party to repent as they are led by the Lord. **We should not apologize in an effort to make the other party apologize, but because we are wrong and want to make things right. A sincere apology will go very far in a relationship.**

Now, let's contrast the approach of David in taking full responsibility with King Saul's. King Saul never once took responsibility for his actions. He always blamed the people and therefore never came into any true repentance. We must take responsibility for our actions. We can't blame someone else for our actions. We must own our actions because it's the godly thing to do. I also must say that if we happen to be in a position of leadership, we should take full responsibility, even for the actions of our subordinates that are done to advance a cause under our oversight.

Pride and self-centeredness are two of the reasons why people refuse to take responsibility for their actions and behavior. They think they are too good to mess up and by accepting any responsibility, it could hurt their reputation and ego. Humble people have no problem admitting they are wrong and taking full responsibility for their own actions.

Do Not Get Mad At God

Now therefore the sword shall never depart from thine house; because thou hast despised me, and hast taken the wife of Uriah the Hittite to be thy wife. Thus saith the LORD, Behold, I will raise up evil against thee out of thine own house, and I will take thy wives before thine eyes, and give them unto thy neighbor, and he shall lie with thy wives in the sight of this sun. For thou didst it secretly: but I will do this thing before all Israel, and before the sun. And David said unto Nathan, I have sinned against the LORD. And Nathan said unto David, The LORD also hath put away thy sin; thou shalt not die. Howbeit, because by this deed thou hast given great occasion to the enemies of the LORD to blaspheme, the child also that is born unto thee shall surely die.

— 2 Samuel 12:10-14

You should not get mad at God, especially if you have inflicted these wounds upon yourself. One other thing we can learn from David is that after he received the judgment and began to see things unfold, starting with the death of his child by Bathsheba, David did not blame God or even get mad at God for the things that were happening. I believe the reason why David never got angry at God was because he had prescribed judgment to the rich man (2 Samuel 12:5-6) in the story Nathan told him and therefore was receiving the same measure of judgment that he had dished out. He also never got mad because he had taken responsibility for his actions.

Thank You, Jesus, that in the New Testament, we will not be judged for our sin because our sins were paid in full by Jesus on the cross, and He took all the judgment we deserved. Thank You, Jesus!

Lack Of Action = Lack Of Leadership

*But when king David heard of all these things, he
was very wroth.*

— 2 Samuel 13:21

David heard that Amnon had raped his own sister
Tamar. He was very displeased and angry, but he did not
do anything about it as the leader of his house and of Israel. Just getting angry and not taking any godly appropriate
action was no help. David was the father and king to both
of these individuals, and he was in position of authority to
render some sort of punishment or discipline for this gross
behavior by Amnon, but David never did a thing.

Although David had committed terrible sins of adultery
and murder, he should have taken some action, exercised
his authority, and rendered some sort of punishment to Amnon. Why did David do nothing? Could he have been fearful of how the people could have perceived his punishment
of Amnon, knowing well what he had done earlier with
Bathsheba and Uriah? Could he have believed that it was
hypocritical on his part to do something to Amnon, yet he
had done something possibly worse? Probably so, but this
was no excuse for him not to act. He was the leader of the
home and the King of Israel, therefore some sort of punishment or discipline was at least expected. Although morally
David had messed up significantly more than Amnon, who
was in the right position to render discipline but David? For
two full years from the time of rape, David took no action
which caused things to get worse. Tamar's brother Absalom

took vengeance into his own hands and plotted to kill Amnon, his half-brother (2 Samuel 13:20-33), but this probably wouldn't have happened had David acted as a real leader ought to act.

This is not to excuse Absalom's behavior, but to make the point that David's lack of action, discipline or punishment of Amnon, eventually led to Absalom's hatred and Amnon's eventual murder. David could have stopped all of this by just taking the appropriate action. He should have cared less about how people would have perceived or viewed it (knowing his sin with Bathsheba and Uriah's murder) and taken action. Some may say, "Well, it's hypocritical for David to have acted in disciplining Amnon." I beg to differ. David would have been doing the right thing as a leader and father regardless of how it would have been viewed by others. He was the one in authority, not anyone else. His lack of action was even worse because it escalated lots of other problems in the family.

Regardless of how many times we have failed as leaders, we should always take steps of action to solve problems, even if we have been guilty of the same. We must repent and humble ourselves and then take action. **We cannot hide our inactivity behind the fact that we have flaws in a similar or certain area.** There would have been a humble way David could have approached this situation and executed punishment had he set his heart to do so. For example, he could have said, "I'm guilty of something like what you have done Amnon, but I repented and humbled myself before the Lord. However, as the man in authority (father and King over Israel), it is my duty and responsibility to render punishment and justice for such unacceptable behavior. When I screwed up, the Lord dealt with me. But when you do, it's my responsibility and job to discipline you." **We should not let our past sins render us ineffective, especially if we are leaders in authority.** If David acted this way, it would have been a deterrent for sin in the future and would have sent a message to others not to act foolishly, knowing he wouldn't shy away from dealing with them.

Although it's true that our lack of moral acuteness affects our influence (leadership), we must still do what is right regardless of how it could be perceived by others, especially those who know our flaws and weaknesses. If you are a leader, you must deal with all issues and all problems even if you are, or once were, guilty of the same. If we are in a position of authority and we do not do something about such things, then that is the definition of true hypocrisy. It is not hypocritical for me to do what is right based on my position of authority, even if I struggled in the same area before. However, it is wisdom that a leader should repent first and have a clear conscience while dealing with a problem in which he was once involved. It is necessary to repent as soon as possible and not take nine months or more like David.

We should not be intimidated into inaction by those who might be watching. **We must do what is right, and a lack of action means a lack of leadership.** We will be respected by those who want to respect us and disrespected by those who have never respected us. Leaders must always confront problems, because if we don't, they will not just go away. Instead, the problems will just multiply down the road. Time cannot heal all wounds; some just get worse over time.

This reminds me of David not dealing with Joab who had killed Abner. This problem returned to David, and stung him. Joab enabled his sin of killing Uriah and later he joined Adonijah to rebel against Solomon. Had David dismissed, disciplined, or dealt with Joab, his future could have had fewer problems. We can learn so much from this part of David's life. David let Amnon off the hook, and for two full years from the time of the rape until he was killed by Absalom, no discipline or punishment was ever given. No action was taken against Amnon for raping Tamar. There should have been no hesitation for disciplining Ammon because this was wrong beyond comprehension.

What was David's thinking, not to act on such a grievous sin? Was he thinking that because God had prophesied tragedy in his house this was part of it, and therefore took no action against it believing it was the "hand of the Lord?" I truly believe that David was "paralyzed" (I'm using this word loosely) from action and good discernment from the day he went into Bathsheba. He lived in denial for so long (imagine two full years of no action).

Later this pattern of lack of action on David's part continued. It cost him his throne, at least temporarily. David knew the dealings of Absalom; how he stole the hearts of the people away from the King (deceptively, of course) and how he planned treason against David (2 Samuel 15), but he again did nothing. I am not convinced that David knew nothing about all of this. There is no way David could not have known. Imagine if it was someone else besides his son who had plotted this treason, how would he have responded?

Besides David knowing about it, David had all the might, forces, and ability to extinguish this treasonous plan. David had conquered bigger and stronger enemies than Absalom, like the Philistines (2 Samuel 19:9). Surely Absalom was no match for David, if he chose to stop this foolishness. He could have crushed Absalom. His inaction led to the deaths of many people due to the war that later broke out between Absalom's army and David's men. David had become passive in his general dealings and behavior.

There was a pattern of inaction that David had developed over time. He had not dealt with Amnon, so now it would require even more courage to deal with Absalom. **Whatever we allow will only increase.** We must put out the fire quickly and immediately. Some could argue that this trouble was already pronounced by God upon David and his house through Nathan (2 Samuel 12). It was going to come regardless of how David resisted and fought it.

For instance, if God said you will die, do you go ahead and kill yourself? Do you do things to destroy your life? After all, God said you will die someday! If God said you will be rich, do you steal, and make it happen through ungodly ways? After all, God said you will be rich! But since we know well that evil doesn't come from God (James 1:13-17), we should resist the devil (James 4:7) and let it not prevail because of some prophecy.

Leaders confront problems; they don't shy, hide, or run from them. Be the leader God has called you to be.

Our Actions Always Affect Others Positively Or Negatively

Moreover the Philistines had yet war again with Israel; and David went down, and his servants with him, and fought against the Philistines: and David waxed faint. And Ishbibenob, which was of the sons of the giant, the weight of whose spear weighed three hundred shekels of brass in weight, he being girded with a new sword, thought to have slain David. But Abishai the son of Zeruiah succored him, and smote the Philistine, and killed him. Then the men of David swore unto him, saying, Thou shalt go no more out with us to battle, that thou quench not the light of Israel. And it came to pass after this, that every hand six fingers, and on every foot six toes, four and twenty in number; and he also was born to the giant. And when he defied Israel, Jonathan the son of Shimea the brother of David slew him. These four were born to the giant in Gath, and fell by the hand of David, and by the hand of his servants.

— 2 Samuel 21:15-22

Many times, we don't pay attention to the fact that our actions can affect others in either positive or negative ways. If we knew and paid attention to that, we would act much better than we do. David's challenge of Goliath the giant later inspired his servants to take on four more giants who threatened and defied Israel. It's a lot easier for people to step out and do something, or believe for something, knowing that it has been done before. When people know something has been done before, it's easier for them to take on the same challenge, should it arise, because they have a point of reference.

In the same way, here in the later stages of David's life, he grew weak to the point that he was advised to stop going out with the men to battle. Ishbibenob the giant was killed by Abishai son of Zeruiah; Saph the other son of the giant was killed by Sibbechai the Hushathite; the Elhanan the son of Jaare-Oregon, a Bethlemite, killed the brother of Goliath the Gittie; and another giant or man of great stature was killed by Jonathan the son of Shimea (David's brother). All four giants were killed by the servants of David. Our actions can either inspire others or cause them to despair. Whenever we take bold steps, we are laying groundwork for others to do the same in the future.

Here is another good example in scripture:

And Jesus arose, and followed him, and so did his disciples. And, behold, a woman, which was diseased with an issue of blood twelve years, came behind him, and touched the hem of his garment.

— Matthew 9:19-20

And when they were gone over, they came into the land of Gennesaret. And when the men of that place had knowledge of him, they sent out into all that country round about, and brought unto him all that were diseased; And besought him that they might only touch the hem of his garment: and as many as touched were made perfectly whole.

— Matthew 14:34-36

The incident of the woman with the issue of blood took place before the incident in Matthew 14:36. The question is, how did the people in Matthew know of the touching of the hem of Jesus' garment? I believe the news spread like wildfire when the woman with the issue of blood got healed by touching the hem of His garment to the point that these people were inspired by her actions to also step out in faith and they were also perfectly made whole.

Quick Repentance And A Sensitive Heart Towards The Lord

And David's heart smote him after that he had numbered the people. And David said unto the LORD, I have sinned greatly in that I have done: and now, I beseech thee, O LORD, take away the iniquity of thy servant; for I have done very foolishly.

— 2 Samuel 24:10

It's always very critical that we are seeking the Lord continually and that we have a heart that is sensitive towards Him. David should have at least have backed out of numbering the people when he got some challenge from Joab (2 Samuel 25:3), or gone to the Lord like he always did earlier in his life. Because David did not do that, he erred greatly against the Lord. **The more sensitive we are to the Lord, the more hardened we get towards sin. And the more sensitive we are towards sin, it's clear that we are hardened or insensitive towards God.**

David's heart had condemned him before when he committed adultery and killed Uriah, but he was so hardened to God to hear His voice, let alone the conviction in his heart. One commendable thing that David did this time when he sinned, unlike other times, was to repent immediately. As soon as his heart bothered him (2 Samuel 24:10), *"David said unto the Lord, I have sinned greatly in that I have done and Now I beseech thee oh Lord, take way the iniquity of thy servant: for I have done very foolishly."*

There are four "I"s in David's repentance, which clearly shows that he took full responsibility for his actions. He never blamed Joab, Satan or the people, like King Saul always did. This was one of the most admirable things about David. He never pointed the finger when he sinned, but took responsibility. He owned his actions and repented of them sooner or later.

When David committed sin with Bathsheba and killed Uriah, he took at least nine months to repent and he did not do so until the prophet Nathan was sent to him by the Lord. How do I know? He repented only after his child was born to Bathsheba.

However, in this sin of numbering the people, David repented swiftly, and this time before a prophet was sent by God to rebuke him and deliver his judgment. This is very commendable, something we can learn and apply in our lives.

The Merciful God

And David said unto Gad, I am in a great strait:
let us fall now into the hand of the LORD; for his
mercies are great: and let me not fall into the hand
of man.

— 2 Samuel 24:14

David had sinned against the Lord by numbering the people. It is clear David knew it was wrong and he also encountered some sort of challenge from Joab and his generals for this act (2 Samuel 24:1-3). When you read 2 Samuel 24:1, it sounds as if it was God who moved David to do the numbering, but if it was God, then why would He punish him for doing so? The answer lies in 1 Chronicles 21:1 which clearly says Satan moved David to do the numbering, which makes perfect sense as to why God punished him.

That said, here is where I want to go: When David was given a choice for his punishment, he chose to fall into the hands of the Lord rather than the hands of men because His mercies are great.

Go and say unto David, Thus saith the LORD, I offer
thee three things; choose thee one of them, that I
may do it unto thee. So Gad came to David, and
told him, and said unto him, Shall seven years of
famine come unto thee in thy land? or wilt thou flee
three months before thine enemies, while they pur-
sue thee? or that there be three days' pestilence in
thy land? now advise, and see what answer I shall re-

turn to him that sent me. And David said unto Gad, I am in a great strait: let us fall now into the hand of the LORD; for his mercies are great: and let me not fall into the hand of man. So the LORD sent a pestilence upon Israel from the morning even to the time appointed: and there died of the people from Dan even to Beer-sheba seventy thousand men.

— 2 Samuel 24:12-15

God is a merciful God even when we have sinned. We should always run to God and prefer to be chastened by Him, rather than man, because God is far more gracious and merciful.

Many people have presented God as a mean God, but David had a different perspective and revelation of God. He knew that there was no one as merciful as God. God is not a mean God. He is a loving and merciful God that even during His rebuke He remains gracious and merciful. Thank You, Lord, for being merciful. Had it not been for You, things would be much worse. Things are still as good as they are because of You. You are kind and gracious.

Motives Of The Heart Versus Actions

And Gad came that day to David, and said unto him, Go up, rear an altar unto the LORD in the threshing floor of Araunah the Jebusite.

— 2 Samuel 24:18

Earlier in 1 Samuel 13:8-9, King Saul was rebuked and rejected for assuming the office of the priest by offering a sacrifice. However, here in 2 Samuel 24:18-19, we see David do the same thing, but he was not rebuked nor rejected by the Lord for it. Was God hypocritical in His actions? Was He playing favorites? Was He a respecter of persons? God forbid! There is a difference between what Saul did and what David did. The difference however is not their actions, but their heart motives.

> But the LORD said unto Samuel, Look not on his countenance, or on the height of his stature; because I have refused him: for the LORD seeth not as man seeth; for man looketh on the outward appearance, but the LORD looketh on the heart.
>
> — 1 Samuel 16:7

Our heart motives are bigger and more important than our actions. This is not to say that we should not act right, but God desires and loves actions driven by good or right heart motives. Saul's heart was always wrong. From day one, he was a man-pleaser (Galatians 1:10). He was more concerned with what the people thought of him than God.

> And Samuel said, What hast thou done? And Saul said, Because **I saw that the people were scattered from me**, and that thou camest not within the days appointed, and that the Philistines gathered themselves together at Michmash;
>
> — 1 Samuel 13:11 (Emphasis Mine)

*And Saul said unto Samuel, I have sinned: for I have transgressed the commandment of the LORD, and thy words: because **I feared the people, and obeyed their voice**.*

— 1 Samuel 15:24 (Emphasis Mine)

*Then he said, I have sinned: yet **honor me now, I pray thee, before the elders of my people, and before Israel**, and turn again with me, that I may worship the LORD thy God.*

— 1 Samuel 15:30 (Emphasis Mine)

Notice that he said because I feared the people—not because I feared the Lord, but the **people**.

Saul's heart was never set to please God. His actions were always driven by the wrong heart motives. David, however, was the exact opposite. He always set his heart to do what was pleasing to the Lord. This doesn't mean he never failed in some areas, but he was a God-pleaser. His heart motives were with humility and obedience towards the Lord.

Two similar actions done by two people are not always the same in the eyes of the Lord because of the motives of the heart, which only God can see. The best example is in giving: the motive with which you give is more important than the gift itself and will determine whether you reap because God looks on the heart.

Costless Sacrifice

And the king said unto Araunah, Nay; but I will sure-
ly buy it of thee at a price: neither will I offer burnt
offerings unto the LORD my God of that which doth
cost me nothing. So, David bought the threshing
floor and the oxen for fifty shekels of silver.

— 2 Samuel 24:24

What good is a "sacrifice" that costs you nothing? Would it even be called a sacrifice? Imagine if Jesus never cost God the Father a thing. That would make mankind of no value to God. The fact that Jesus cost the Father so much is a testimony to how much God values and loves us. He could have given a bull to die in our place, or maybe another man, but that would not have placed a tremendous value on us as God giving His only Son Jesus Christ, God manifest in the flesh. A true sacrifice must have a cost to it. No cost means no sacrifice.

Knowing the splendor and majesty that the Lord Jesus Christ gave up for us speaks volumes of how much He values and loves us. God placed a very high value on us and He gave up Heaven for us all. Although Jesus was a gift to us, He was not free from God's perspective because He cost Him Heaven and Earth.

David taught us a very good lesson that many of us need to implement and apply in our lives. He refused to give God an offering that cost him zero. It's one thing to give something you have been given for free. It's another thing to give something that has cost you. It takes a hearty and conscious effort to give something that cost you something. We should not give God "welfare money," but that which has cost us something. Such an offering is more pleasing and it also portrays the very heart of God who gave us His ONLY Son (John 3:16 and Romans 8:32). Another example is the widow who gave her only two mites (Luke 21:2-3). Her giving was sacrificial because it was all she had. Jesus said that she gave more than all that gave that day including rich men. Her heart was right which pleased the Lord.

What a great attitude David had! This man saw things differently from the way other people did because he always sought to be right with God. Contrast this with King Saul, who wanted to offer animals that were supposed to be killed (1 Samuel 15) in the place of his animals from his own flock. David wanted to honor the Lord by placing value on Him. If His sacrifice cost him one million dollars, he would gladly offer it at a cost that much than to offer that which cost him nothing. Your offering or sacrifice indirectly places value on God in your own eyes. Is God worth a dollar to you? Is He worth $100 or $100,000 to you? Or is He worth "free" (zero) to you. The cost of what we give ascribes value to who we give it to. David was determined not to offer a thing which cost him nothing which would translate to ascribing a "zero-dollar price tag" to God. David honored, valued, and esteemed God by offering Him that which cost him, not that which was free.

This is not to say that you should not give a tithe or offering on the money you have been given for free, but to always seek to put a price value on God by our offering and develop a similar attitude like David. If the only time you give is when you have received free money, something is wrong with that attitude. You should give whether it came free or not. The Lord is looking more at your motives and attitudes of the heart than your gift.

The life of David was very interesting. It is the longest life of a king that we have in scripture (excluding King Jesus). We can learn what to do and what not to do from David's life. There were plenty of positives and negatives in David's life, but he still came out as one of the best standards and the godliest king in Israel. He was by no means a sinless man, but God called him a man after His own heart.

Other Kings

King Jehu, Manasseh, Josiah, Saul, and Jehoshaphat

King Jehu
(2 Kings 9-10)

And he arose, and went into the house; and he poured the oil on his head, and said unto him, Thus saith the LORD God of Israel, I have anointed thee king over the people of the LORD, even over Israel. And thou shalt smite the house of Ahab thy master, that I may avenge the blood of my servants the prophets, and the blood of all the servants of the LORD, at the hand of Jezebel.

— 2 Kings 9:6-7

And the LORD said unto Jehu, Because thou hast done well in executing that which is right in mine eyes, and hast done unto the house of Ahab according to all that was in mine heart, thy children of the fourth generation shall sit on the throne of Israel. But Jehu took no heed to walk in the law of the LORD God of Israel with all his heart: for he departed not from the sins of Jeroboam, which made Israel to sin.

— 2 Kings 10:30-31

Jehu was one of the other godliest kings in scripture. There is a lot to learn from his life. Just like David, he made some mistakes, but overall he was a godly king. There are two different things we can learn from the lives of others: what to do and what not to do.

Jehu was supposed to be anointed king by Elijah, but Elijah did not do it. So, Elisha, Elijah's successor, anointed him.

One of the main assignments of Jehu was to avenge the blood of the prophets and all the servants of the Lord at the hand of Jezebel (2 Kings 9:7). He was to destroy the whole house of Ahab (2 Kings 9:8-9). We should learn to let the Lord avenge us. The Lord is the best avenger. If we do it ourselves, then the Lord cannot avenge us. The Word of God teaches that vengeance is the Lords (Romans 12:19 and Hebrews 10:30). A lot of evil had been done by the house of Ahab, but the Lord was determined not to let the house of Ahab and Jezebel get away unpunished.

> And he arose, and went into the house; and he poured the oil on his head, and said unto him, Thus saith the LORD God of Israel, I have anointed thee king over the people of the LORD, even over Israel. And thou shalt smite the house of Ahab thy master, that I may avenge the blood of my servants the prophets, and the blood of all the servants of the LORD, at the hand of Jezebel.
>
> — 2 Kings 9:6-7

King Jehu started his assignment by killing King Joram, son of Ahab, as well as Ahaziah. He slew all that remained of the house of Ahab in Jezreel, all his great men, his kinfolks and his priests, until he left none remaining.

> And the LORD said unto Jehu, Because thou hast done well in executing that which is right in mine eyes, and hast done unto the house of Ahab according to all that was in mine heart, thy children of the fourth generation shall sit on the throne of Israel.
>
> — 2 Kings 10:30

King Jehu did what was pleasing to the Lord, and He was rewarded. There is great reward in obeying the Lord. A reward for good performance is not legalism. We have to reward good performance to encourage good performance.

But 2 Kings 10:31 brings up one of the most outstanding things we can learn from the life of King Jehu: *"But Jehu took no heed to walk in the law of the LORD God of Israel with all his heart: for he departed not from the sins of Jeroboam, which made Israel to sin."*

a) King Jehu took no heed to walk in the Law of the Lord God of Israel with **all** his heart. This clearly implies that he partially sought the Lord. He was not fully devoted.

b) *"He departed not from the sins of Jeroboam which made Israel to sin."* What sins? He held onto the golden calves Jeroboam had made. This defies logic! This man continued to worship the golden images erected by Jeroboam, yet he went on to destroy the Baal worshipers and the evil house of Ahab. This is hypocrisy! All his zeal seemed to be without knowledge.

We can't just partially seek the Lord. We must do it wholeheartedly. One of the reasons that people do not see God manifest in their lives is because they do not do it with **all** their hearts.

Jeremiah 29:12-13 says *"Then shall ye call upon me, and ye shall go and pray unto me, and I will hearken unto you. And ye shall seek me, and find me, when ye shall search for me with all your heart."*

King Manasseh
(2 Chronicles 33-36 and 2 Kings 21)

Manasseh was a very evil and ungodly king for most of his life. He made his son pass through fire, observed times and used enchantments, and dealt with familiar spirits and wizards (2 Kings 21:6). Manasseh built altars for all the hosts of heaven in the two courts of the house of the Lord. He caused the children of Israel to pass through the fire in the valley of the son of Hinnom.

He seduced Israel and caused her to do more evil than the nations whom the Lord destroyed in front of the children of Israel. He would not hearken unto the prophets God sent him. Jewish tradition and some scholars believe that Manasseh had the prophet Isaiah sawed apart. This is possibly referenced in Hebrews 11:37.

It's a shame when people who do not know God live with more morality than those that have a relationship with Him (2 Kings 21:9). 2 Chronicles 33:9 states that *"Manasseh made Judah and the inhabitants of Jerusalem to err, and to do worse than the heathen, whom the Lord had destroyed before the children of Israel."* He shed innocent blood.

However, at the end of his reign, he came to the end of himself when he was conquered and taken into Babylonian captivity (2 Chronicles 33:10-13). It was there that he suffered severely and eventually humbled himself, repented, and got restored to his kingdom in Judah (2 Chronicles 33:12-16). Despite all the evil that Manasseh did, when he humbled himself greatly before the Lord and prayed unto

Him, the Lord heard his supplication and brought him back to his kingdom (2 Chronicles 33:9-13).

The most wicked of all the kings of Judah repented of his idolatry and turned to serve and follow the only true God. **Why should we wait for bad times to stop doing what's wrong and turn to the Lord?**

There is not one heart that the Lord cannot turn, touch, heal, or save if they will only humble ourselves, repent, and believe on Him. It's very simple. In Manasseh, we see what God can do in and through a man who will greatly humble himself regardless of what he has done. God can even save and forgive the so-called greatest sinner out there, just like He did for King Manasseh.

Although Manasseh was restored to his kingdom, we must learn that forgiveness does not necessarily call for full restoration, privileges, and trust. These things have to be earned afresh if they have been lost. Many times, someone can be forgiven and loved, yet not restored to their previous position. Forgiveness and restoration are not synonymous.

Amon, Manasseh's son, never learned good from his father, but only evil. He did not humble himself before the LORD, as Manasseh his father had humbled himself (2 Chronicles 33:24).

We cannot live holy or godly without any effort towards that direction. At the same time, we do not need a lot of effort to live ungodly. It's easier to grow weeds than to grow corn. It's easier to pass on evil to our children and other people than to pass on goodness and godliness. It's easier to be sick than to be healed. It's easier to be fat than to be skinny. Sickness is contagious, but health is not. Amon easily picked up on the evil of his father Manasseh, rather than his eventual goodness, humility, and repentance.

Manasseh went on to destroy the very altars he had built and took the idols out of the house of the Lord. He commanded the children of Israel to serve the Lord. The people still sacrificed in the high places, but only unto the Lord their God.

King Josiah
(2 Chronicles 34 and 2 Kings 22)

King Josiah was another godly king. *"He did what was right in the sight of the Lord, and walked in the ways of David, his father, and declined neither to the right hand nor to the left"* (2 Chronicles 34:2). In the eighth year of his reign, while he was still young (16 years old), he began to seek after the God of David. In the twelfth year, he began to purge Judah and Jerusalem of the high places, the groves, carved images, and molten images (2 Chronicles 34:3). We should not wait to seek the Lord when we are old. We must do so starting at a young age like King Josiah.

Remember now thy Creator in the days of thy youth, while the evil days come not, nor the years draw nigh, when thou shalt say, I have no pleasure in them.

—Ecclesiastes 12:1

King Josiah broke down the altars of Baalim in his presence and the images that were on high above them he cut down, and the groves. He took the carved images and the molten images and broke them in pieces.

Zealous for the things of God, He went on to repair the house of the Lord and in the process of doing so, he discovered the Book of the Law of the Lord given by Moses. He took away all the abominations out of all the countries that pertained to the children of Israel and made all of them that were present in Israel serve the Lord their God.

During all his reign, Israel did not depart from following the Lord, the God of their fathers (2 Chronicles 34:33). Josiah was very diligent, and under his watch, Israel sought the Lord because of his leadership.

Josiah kept the Passover—something that many kings did not do before him. There was no Passover like that kept in Israel from the days of Samuel the prophet; neither did all the kings of Israel keep such a Passover as Josiah did. Josiah was doing well up until the point where he wanted to go to war with Necho, yet Necho was not at war with him. He insisted and went to fight Necho, which resulted in his defeat, injury, and subsequent death (2 Chronicles 35:20-27).

This was a grave mistake on Josiah's part. He had earlier received a good prophecy about his peaceful death, but the prophecy that the Prophetess Huldah gave about his peaceful death did not come to pass because it required his cooperation. It was conditional. Most prophecies are conditional even when the condition is not clearly stated. Fulfillment of

God's Word or promise can be dependent on our cooperation even when it's not clearly spelled out.

Josiah went against God's will to fight with Pharaoh-Necho, the king of Egypt, and he died in the battle contrary to God's prophecy through Huldah (2 Chronicles 34:28; 35:20-24 and 2 Kings 22:20).

Even a man who sought God from his childhood made some mistakes. This makes a point that God does not have anyone qualified to work for Him, and you and I won't be the first ones. Josiah was one of the kings that God spoke highly of. True greatness comes when we honor God—not the world and the things it offers.

We learn that righteousness cannot be inherited from father to son. Manasseh was evil and so was his son Amon. But Josiah, the son of Amon, did that which was right in the sight of God. He chose a totally different route than his father and grandfather. He chose godliness; he sought after the Lord.

As a side note, we also learn from Huldah the prophetess that God uses women, too (2 Kings 22:14-17). Huldah was a prophetess that God used during the reign of King Josiah. Some people have a problem with seeing women being used by God. One of the reasons is because they have misinterpreted certain scriptures such as 1 Timothy 2:12. There are several women in the Bible that were prophetesses: Miriam the sister of Moses (Exodus 15:20), Deborah (Judges 4:4), Anna (Luke 2), and the four daughters who did prophecy (Acts 21:9).

The Bible says there was none like Josiah (2 Kings 23:25). We also learn that when King Josiah had men work for him, he paid them. They never worked for nothing (2 Kings 22:1-7). It's ungodly to use people and not pay them. We also should not be cheap, or pay cheaply.

Josiah started seeking the Lord at an early age. His love for the Lord, his zeal, and his passion are very commendable. He is yet another example of a godly man we can learn from.

King Saul

And it came to pass, when Samuel was old, that he made his sons judges over Israel. Now the name of his firstborn was Joel; and the name of his second, Abiah: they were judges in Beersheba. And his sons walked not in his ways, but turned aside after lucre, and took bribes, and perverted judgment. When all the elders of Israel gathered themselves together, and came to Samuel unto Ramah, And said unto him, Behold, thou art old, and thy sons walk not in thy ways: now make us a king to judge us like all the nations. But the thing displeased Samuel, when they said, Give us a king to judge us. And Samuel prayed unto the Lord.

—1 Samuel 8:1-6

King Saul comes on the scene after the children of Israel demand for a king. Israel was looking at other nations and wanted to be like them. At this point, God was the King over Israel and He reigned through judges and prophets. The future would-be judges were the sons of Samuel. Unfortunately, they proved to be ungodly, and Samuel was old.

The elders started saying that Samuel was old, which was an excuse, and tried to press forward with their desire to have their own king apart from the Lord. I believe Samuel could still perform his duties as a prophet, and we see that he lived on almost through King Saul's reign. These elders were playing the "age card." They had two excuses as to why they should walk away from God. One, "Samuel, you are old." Two, "your sons are ungodly."

Notice, it displeased Samuel that they desired a king (1 Samuel 8:6). Samuel could not be fooled by the reasons these elders had given. He saw right through their so-called "desire to have a king." He knew that their hearts weren't right. It was not because he was old or that his sons were ungodly, but because they desired a king.

Samuel inquired of the Lord and God revealed to him that this rejection was not a rejection of Samuel, but a rejection of the Lord. God revealed the heart condition of the Israelites. They were done having God reign over them. They wanted to be like the world and all other nations. Their hearts were not right.

In 1 Samuel 8:8, God says that their hearts were going after serving other gods and they had been doing so since they came out of Egypt. We can learn that people are not always sincere in their demands. Looking deeper, you will discover a different motive and agenda. We must shoot for the root and not the leaves. What is the reason why people ask for what they ask for? Do not be fooled by what people say on the surface, but try to find out by inquiring of the Lord or even asking them personally. People will rarely be straightforward with their demands without masking them in some sort of excuse. Beware! President Ronald Reagan once said, *"Trust, but verify."*

Rejecting God's Leadership = Rejecting God

But the thing displeased Samuel, when they said, Give us a king to judge us. And Samuel prayed unto the Lord.

And the Lord said unto Samuel, Hearken unto the voice of the people in all that they say unto thee: for they have not rejected thee, but they have rejected me, that I should not reign over them."

—1 Samuel 8:6-7

When people start moving away and wanting to part from the Lord, it is because their heart is not right. The problem is a heart issue.

God told Samuel to hearken to the voice of the people. God was not delighted in giving them their desired king, but He had respect for their will and gave them their choice.

This was not God's perfect will, yet He granted it mainly because of their will and the hardness of the people's hearts.

God may give us what we want, but it doesn't mean it is His perfect will for us. We must let God give us His desires (Psalm 37:4). He will put His desires in our hearts and they will be in line with His, and He will therefore easily bring them to pass. We should not tell God what to do, but we must submit ourselves to what He wants to do.

Later, God started to elaborate what would happen when they were under their desired king. They were going to suffer under this king and pay a huge price for their demand for him. God saw what was coming ahead of everyone else and shared it upfront. He was not going to inspire this bad behavior, but He saw it ahead of time and told them what would happen.

Foreknowledge is not synonymous to predetermination. God foresaw this, but did not cause it. He was just warning the people of what awaited them once this king was installed. I am thinking of an example where a parent told a child that if he went outside the house, he would be eaten by a lion. The parent could foresee the danger, but did not determine it. If I told you that if you jumped off a cliff you would die, and you went against my advice, jumped, and died—I cannot be blamed for causing your death, even though I foresaw it. I'm not the bad guy. Apparently, you are.

These Israelites had no idea what they had demanded. There were about to become servants of another man. This was not going to be pretty.

These people were so sold on their desire to have a king that they refused to heed the voice of the Lord. They were blinded by their so-called desires, but this again points back to their heart condition. The king they were demanding was going to bring tears, not joy. This king would take a tenth of their sheep, their seed, etc. He would make their men servants and their women maids. They were better off having God as their King instead of another man, and in this case, King Saul.

The Selection of Saul

And the asses of Kish Saul's father were lost. And Kish said to Saul his son, Take now one of the servants with thee, and arise, go seek the asses. And he passed through mount Ephraim, and passed through the land of Shalisha, but they found them not: then they passed through the land of Shalim, and there they were not: and he passed through the land of the Benjamites, but they found them not. And when they were come to the land of Zuph, Saul said to his servant that was with him, Come, and let us return; lest my father leave caring for the asses, and take thought for us.

— 1 Samuel 9:3-5

Then Samuel took a vial of oil, and poured it upon his head, and kissed him, and said, Is it not because the Lord hath anointed thee to be captain over his inheritance?

—1 Samuel 10:1

And when Samuel had caused all the tribes of Israel to come near, the tribe of Benjamin was taken. When he had caused the tribe of Benjamin to come near by their families, the family of Matri was taken, and Saul the son of Kish was taken: and when they sought him, he could not be found. Therefore they enquired of the Lord further, if the man should yet come thither. And the Lord answered, Behold he hath hid himself among the stuff. And they ran and fetched him thence: and when he stood among the people, he was higher than any of the people from his shoulders and upward. And Samuel said to all the people, See ye him whom the Lord hath chosen, that there is none like him among all the people? And all the people shouted, and said, God save the king.

—1 Samuel 10:20-24

Saul's journey to reigning as king over Israel began when he lost his asses and started looking for them, but could not find them. His servant told him about an honorable prophet to seek out for help because his word always came to pass.

And he said unto him, Behold now, there is in this city a man of God, and he is an honourable man; all that he saith cometh surely to pass: now let us go thither; peradventure he can shew us our way that we should go.

—1 Samuel 9:6

The prophet Samuel had a good reputation. He was very honorable and respected. God was leading the nation of Israel through Samuel. There was no king at this time.

When Saul and his servant came to him, just like his reputation was, he did not disappoint. *"And as for thine asses that were lost three days ago, set not thy mind on them; for they are found. And on whom is all the desire of Israel? Is it not on thee, and on all thy father's house?"* (1 Samuel 9:20)

The Lord can reveal things to us ahead of time through the Holy Spirit. He did with prophet Samuel under the Old Testament (1 Samuel 9:15-16). How much more under the New Testament? Also, I should mention that Saul was at the right place in the right time, but so was Samuel. Samuel continually received words of knowledge from the Lord. The Lord speaks and He shows us things to come (John 16:13), but notice that He doesn't show us **all** things to come; I believe that if He did, how would we then walk by faith?

Samuel began to read Saul's mail. Before Saul even said he was looking for his asses, Samuel helped him "cool his jets" of fear, revealing to him that they were found and also that he was the desire (king) of Israel. In other words, he was the king-to-be that Israel yearned for. Saul then began to talk of how inferior and unworthy he was, pointing back to his family and background. He was immediately elevated to eat with Samuel in the highest places and the next morning Samuel anointed him king over Israel.

Later, Samuel would to say that Saul would meet men prophesying and God would give him another heart and **"the spirit of the Lord will come upon him and he shall be turned into another man" (1 Samuel 10:6)**. God gave Saul another heart. From this point he was never to be the same man.

We all need a change of heart to pursue God's will for our lives (John 3:3). Saul needed another heart to accomplish what God had called him to do, but this does not mean that God took away his free will. Although we later see the failure of Saul, it was not because of a lack of God's support.

In the Old Testament, the Spirit came upon people, but in the New Testament, the Spirit is living in us and always upon us. He never leaves us. Also, when we get baptized in the Holy Spirit, we are turned into "another man." We completely become driven, possessed, led and controlled by the Holy Spirit **as we yield to Him**.

Saul was given a new heart and had the Holy Spirit come upon him. Just like Saul, we also need both. You must be born again (John 3:3) and be filled with the Holy Spirit (Acts 1:8) to live a victorious Christian life. The Lord wanted to work through Saul, but Saul had to cooperate with Him through obedience.

Samuel instructed Saul to go down to Gilgal and he would come down to offer burnt offerings and to make sacrifices of peace and burnt offerings. He instructed him to wait for seven days until he showed up to show him what to do.

And thou shalt go down before me to Gilgal; and, behold, I will come down unto thee, to offer burnt offerings, and to sacrifice sacrifices of peace offerings: seven days shalt thou tarry, till I come to thee, and shew thee what thou shalt do."

—1 Samuel 10:8

Note: (This occurrence is different from the 1 Samuel 11:14-15.)

Later, at the time of his inauguration, Saul went missing. He hid because he was afraid. He hid from men, but not from God. God knew exactly where he was and told the leaders. We can lie to men, hide from men, we can do all these things to men, but not to God. God sees and knows everything. Just ask Saul.

God touched the hearts of the people. Why would God do so when a king for Israel was not His perfect will? This was something permissible, but not His perfect will for Israel. Since He had anointed Saul to be king, He did not anoint him to fail, but to succeed and accomplish His will: therefore, He touched the hearts of the people.

Rebuke For Desiring A King

Now therefore hearken unto their voice: howbeit yet protest solemnly unto them, and shew them the manner of the king that shall reign over them. And Samuel told all the words of the Lord unto the people that asked of him a king. And he said, This will be the manner of the king that shall reign over you: He will take your sons, and appoint them for himself, for his chariots, and to be his horsemen; and some shall run before his chariots. And he will appoint him captains over thousands, and captains over fifties; and will set them to ear his ground, and to reap his harvest, and to make his instruments of war, and instruments of his

*chariots. And he will take your daughters to be con-
fectionaries, and to be cooks, and to be bakers. And
he will take your fields, and your vineyards, and your
oliveyards, even the best of them, and give them to
his servants. And he will take the tenth of your seed,
and of your vineyards, and give to his officers, and
to his servants. And he will take your menservants,
and your maidservants, and your goodliest young
men, and your asses, and put them to his work. He
will take the tenth of your sheep: and ye shall be his
servants. And ye shall cry out in that day because
of your king which ye shall have chosen you; and
the Lord will not hear you in that day."*

—1 Samuel 8:9-18

Although the Lord gave them their desired king, they also received a rebuke from Him through Samuel. The rebuke and warning they received from God clearly indicates that this was not God's will for Israel—at least not His perfect will. In the process of having a king, they were supposed to obey the Lord or risk His hand against them. They were going to be consumed if they did wickedly along with their king.

Here is something to learn: God's permissible will for a king was accompanied by a strong warning and a rebuke. We should desire to be in God's perfect will. The Lord rebukes us because He loves us. *"Thou shalt not hate thy brother in thine heart: thou shalt in any wise rebuke thy neighbor, and not suffer sin upon him"* (Leviticus 19:17).

The children of Israel did not know what they were asking for. Had they known what 1 Samuel 8:9-18 said about their desired king, they would have restrained their request for a king. This was not a wise move. They were better off having God as their King, not a man.

The children of Israel were going to be enslaved, and they were going to pay a price for desiring this king which was not God's perfect will for them.

How many times do we ask for what we do not even know? The best course of action would be to ask God for what He wants us to have if we really need something that we desire. Not every desire we have is a godly desire. In this case, the desire of the children of Israel was not of God. It was entirely selfish and born out of comparison. They desired so much to be like the "world" to the point that they rejected the Lord. This is no different to what happens to us today. We tend to look at others and ask God for things that others have, not knowing what we are asking for. Many times we think what we desire is going to make us better, but to our surprise, it is the very opposite. We are instead enslaved, troubled and destroyed by such things. We should instead ask God to give us the desires of His own heart (Pslam 37:4).

Falling...

During Saul's second year of reigning, he started making mistakes. His fear of men and the desire to please people got him to do what was wrong. He started to value and esteem people's opinions above God's.

There came a time when the Philistines were before him and the people were in hiding (1 Samuel 13:6-7). Saul was under pressure, he waited for Samuel for seven days according to the time set, but he came not in the appointed time. So, when the people scattered, Saul panicked.

Saul was anointed king, not prophet. It was wrong for him to assume and operate in the office of priest or prophet because he was not anointed to operate in these offices. It's interesting that when he took on this office to offer sacrifice, as soon as he had finished, Samuel showed up. If only Saul had waited a little longer! Samuel was just around the corner. If we can't wait for a minute, we should stand for two more because our victory is just around the corner.

This brings out what 1 Corinthians 10:13 says, *"There hath no temptation taken you but such as is common to man: but God is faithful, who will not suffer you to be tempted above that ye are able; but will with the temptation also make a way to escape, that ye may be able to bear it."*

There is no situation that comes our way that we cannot endure or overcome. Now, this may sound too radical for some people, but that's the truth. If you face it, God has provided the grace for you to overcome it. If it so happens that you are going to be overrun or overcome by it, God will supernaturally intervene and provide a way of escape.

Saul thought he could not wait any longer. But then, within no time, Samuel arrived. I have to ask this question: Did Samuel delay on purpose or did God cause this delay to expose Saul's heart? How many times have we been unfaithful and impatient and then our breakthrough comes right after we've screwed things up? If you can't wait any longer—wait!

King Saul blew it. He messed up, and Samuel was not pleased. On the surface, it seemed as though Samuel was wrong for showing up late, but even if he was, it doesn't justify King Saul's actions of offering burnt offerings. This was not his office or his calling. He was King, not priest. But in addition to that, his heart was not right even in offering the burnt offering. Saul never accepted responsibility for his actions. He blamed Samuel and the people—Samuel for coming late, and the people for scattering from him.

Actually, the key issue here was not that Samuel came not in the appointed time, but that Saul was a man-pleaser. He sought to please man even if it meant disobeying God. This was so wrong. This man had a problem—a huge problem. *"The fear of man bringeth a snare: but whoso putteth his trust in the LORD shall be safe"* (Proverbs 29:25).

King Saul knew very well that offering these burnt offerings was wrong, and it was not his office, yet he went ahead and did it anyway. What does this say about Saul? Saul never valued or esteemed God. He did all that seemed good to himself. He forced himself to do it. He had reservations and convictions from the Holy Spirit in his heart, yet he ignored all of that and did as he wanted. We should be very cautious not to do things we have reservations for. **If we have doubts, we should never force ourselves. We should never go against the conviction of the Holy Spirit in our hearts.** Every time we go against the conviction in our hearts (Romans 2:15) or any reservations we have, we end up committing sin. Another good example here is in 2 Chronicles 18:2, when King Jehoshaphat was persuaded to go with King Ahab and fight against Ramoth-gilead. For him to be persuaded, it had to be against his convictions. He clearly had reservations against this. This is further proved by him asking to inquire of the prophet of the Lord.

Saul paid heavily for his actions in the name of pleasing people. 1 Samuel 13:13 reveals another powerful truth. Because of Saul's disobedience, the kingdom was taken from him. But notice what the LORD said, *"…for now would the Lord have established thy kingdom, upon Israel, forever."* God's original plan was to establish the kingdom, or the throne of Israel, forever through King Saul. Had Saul been faithful, we would never have heard of David. God was willing to keep Saul as His man even if He was not in favor of Israel having a king in the first place. In other words, Saul was God's plan A and yet it never turned out well. It fell flat on its face!

We can learn God's will doesn't always come to pass. One of the reasons is because it involves and requires man's cooperation, which sometimes doesn't happen. God had to come up with a second choice (David) which turned out to be a far better plan than His first choice (Saul). We also learn that not all the promises of God are unconditional; some are conditional.

Samuel continued and said that the kingdom of Saul would not continue because the LORD had sought a man after His own heart. King Saul continued to be king for about thirty-eight years, but the throne lineage had changed houses to that of David.

Someone can look at this and say, where is God's grace? God's grace is in the mercy for Israel as a whole in that He protected them from the tragedy of King Saul. If King Saul was not dismissed, Israel would have been worse off. The Lord had to do something with Saul for the sake of Israel as a whole. Now, that's grace!

We should never use the grace of God to be disrespectful towards God. The grace of God empowers us to live godly lives, not to give excuses for ungodly lives (Titus 2:11-12). We can't hide behind grace as an excuse to disobey God. Disobedience can stop God from using us greatly in the way He would like. We determine how much God can use us by how much we are cooperating with Him. God is not going to promote laziness, dishonesty, and disobedience. We must cooperate with Him.

We must learn to take responsibility for our actions. We can't blame someone else for our failure, even if they failed too. **You cannot take another person's behavior, good or bad, to excuse your own actions. We must do what is right regardless of how other people act.**

One of King Saul's greatest problems was pride. He made himself the center of the universe. He was very selfish and self-centered. Saul never took responsibility for anything. He made many grave mistakes, but his arrogance and the fear of men caused him to never be humble before the Lord.

And when the people were come into the wood, behold, the honey dropped; but no man put his hand to his mouth: for the people feared the oath. But Jonathan heard not when his father charged the people with the oath: wherefore he put forth the end of the rod that was in his hand, and dipped it in an honeycomb, and put his hand to his mouth;

and his eyes were enlightened. Then answered one of the people, and said, Thy father straitly charged the people with an oath, saying, Cursed be the man that eateth any food this day. And the people were faint. Then said Jonathan, My father hath troubled the land: see, I pray you, how mine eyes have been enlightened, because I tasted a little of this honey.

—1 Samuel 14:26-29

He later goes to war with the Philistines after he knew of the slaughter that Jonathan, his son and his armor bearer, had wrought by slaying a garrison of Philistines. Saul claimed victory and took his army to continue the slaughter, but he also made an oath that they should not eat a thing that day of war until later and warned that whosoever did eat would die.

The people were faint because they had not eaten and when time came to eat, they ate with blood, thereby sinning against the Lord. However, Jonathan his son, who was away at the time of this oath, ate a little honey, not aware of the oath his father had made. Because of this Saul wanted to kill Jonathan. And he would have, had it not been for the people who intervened. *"And the people said unto Saul, Shall Jonathan die, who hath wrought this great salvation in Israel? God forbid: as the Lord liveth, there shall not one hair of his head fall to the ground; for he hath wrought with God this day. So the people rescued Jonathan, that he died not"* (1 Samuel 14:45). Again, this was something silly, but the people weren't very pleased with Saul's evil desire. Jonathan was supposed to be rewarded for killing the Philistines, but Saul wanted to kill him in the name of this oath and eating a little honey.

Again, instead of Saul humbling himself and saying he was wrong, he refused and wanted to kill his son. These people had more sense and they rejected his advances. They weren't in agreement with him killing Jonathan. Therefore, the people rescued Jonathan.

This battle was supposed to wipe the Philistines out completely, but how could this happen with such leadership from King Saul? The people were so weak because they had not eaten all day. Saul was a terrible leader, and the same people he let off the hook later killed him and his three sons. Saul went on to build an altar unto the Lord, yet he was not permitted to do so. Once Saul started sinning against the Lord, he never stopped.

> *Samuel also said unto Saul, The Lord sent me to anoint thee to be king over his people, over Israel: now therefore hearken thou unto the voice of the words of the Lord. Thus saith the Lord of hosts, I remember that which Amalek did to Israel, how he laid wait for him in the way, when he came up from Egypt. Now go and smite Amalek, and utterly destroy all that they have, and spare them not; but slay both man and woman, infant and suckling, ox and sheep, camel and ass.*
>
> —1 Samuel 15:1-3

But like we all know, God is a God of second chances. He gave Saul yet another opportunity to right his wrongs this time around, but he blew it as well. Samuel went to Saul and gave him instructions from the Lord to go and utterly destroy the Amalekites. He was to slay man, woman, infant and suckling, ox and sheep, camel and ass.

God wanted to avenge the Israelites of what the Amalekites had done to them earlier. King Saul went to take care of business, but his obedience was only partial. Partial obedience equals disobedience. He disobeyed the voice of the Lord and yet again did his own thing. You couldn't just tell Saul what to do—not even God could. So, King Saul smote everything else but spared King Agag of the Amalekites, the best of the sheep, the oxen and the fatlings, and the lambs and would not utterly destroy them as commanded by God through Samuel. So God revealed to Samuel what Saul had done, and he went out to meet him the next morning. King Saul came to meet Samuel pleased with himself, that he had performed the Word of the Lord. This man was more like a reprobate. He had lost the sense of what was right and wrong. He could not even see that he had missed it. He was so hardened and could not even distinguish between right and wrong. This is what sin does to us. He had not utterly destroyed everything. When he got confronted by Samuel, he blamed the people. He refused to take responsibility, yet again. The instructions were given to him, yet he blamed the people. You can't find an incident where Saul ever took responsibility.

And Samuel said, Hath the LORD as great delight in burnt offerings and sacrifices, as in obeying the voice of the LORD? Behold, to obey is better than sacrifice, and to hearken than the fat of rams. For rebellion is as the sin of witchcraft, and stubbornness is as iniquity and idolatry. Because thou hast

rejected the word of the LORD, he hath also reject-
ed thee from being king.

—1 Samuel 15:22-23

He chose to sacrifice rather than to obey the commandment of the Lord (1 Samuel 15:2). Rejecting God's Word equals rejecting God. Disobedience and rebellion against God is witchcraft, and stubbornness is as idolatry.

King Saul forgot his humble beginning and chose not to follow God. 1 Samuel 15:24 says that he feared the people and obeyed their voice. This man chose not to fear God who made him king over Israel. What a shame! Lord, help me not to walk in the fear of men.

And Saul said unto Samuel, I have sinned: for I have transgressed the commandment of the LORD, and thy words: because I feared the people, and obeyed their voice. Now therefore, I pray thee, pardon my sin, and turn again with me, that I may worship the LORD. And Samuel said unto Saul, I will not return with thee: for thou hast rejected the word of the LORD, and the LORD hath rejected thee from being king over Israel. And as Samuel turned about to go away, he laid hold upon the skirt of his mantle, and it rent. And Samuel said unto him, The LORD hath rent the kingdom of Israel from thee this day, and hath given it to a neighbor of thine, that is better than thou. And also the Strength of Israel will not lie nor repent: for he is not a man, that he should repent. Then he said, I have sinned: yet honor me now, I pray thee, before the elders of my people, and before Israel, and turn again with me, that I may worship the LORD thy God.

— 1 Samuel 15:24-30

Because of all this, God rejected King Saul. I also must say clearly that King Saul rejected God first, so God took the kingdom from him and gave it to his neighbor, David. Saul went further and asked Samuel to honor him publicly so that the people would not forsake him. This is the way Saul lived. He always wanted to be seen of men. He was not even bothered by God's rejection. All he wanted was to be honored before the elders and Israel. "Who cares about God?" he probably thought.

Saul was a very insecure man. He continually sought the approval of people. He valued people's opinions over God's opinion. What a bad example of a leader!

Takeaways From King Saul

One - Never go against your heart. Never force yourself. Never go against the conviction of the Holy Spirit. If you have any reservations, against anything, do not just do it, but rather sleep on it, or put it on the shelf until later. We have to go against our heart reservations and convictions to sin.

Two - Disobedience doesn't release blessings. Saul's disobedience cost him his kingdom.

Three - Never be a man-pleaser. You will end up disobeying God. It is impossible to please God and man at the same time (Galatians 1:10). Who will you choose to please?

Four - God's plans are dependent on us. Our cooperation is crucial for God's will to come to pass. God's plans are not infallible. We must cooperate with God to see and eat the good of the land.

Five - Take responsibility for your actions and do not blame someone else for your failures.

Six - We should stay humble and God-dependent, even when things get better. The greatest temptation for man is success, power, wealth, and prosperity. We must keep our eyes fixed on Jesus.

King Jehoshaphat
(2 Chronicles 17-20)

King Jehoshaphat was another one of the godliest kings that we read about in the Bible. Although there are lots of good things about his life that we can learn from and apply to our lives, there are also things in his life that we want to stay away from. There was no perfect king, but surely some had a heart for the Lord more than others. Some intentionally sought the Lord more than others.

His father, King Asa, was a man who loved the Lord and sought the Lord. *"And Asa did that which was right in the eyes of the LORD, as did David his father"* (1 Kings 15:11). King Jehoshaphat walked in the ways of the Lord as his father and did that which was right in the eyes of God (1 Kings 22:43). We see that our behavior can inspire our children to follow a godly path, but it doesn't happen automatically. I believe that King Asa played a major role to personally help steer the life of his son Jehoshaphat towards godliness and the love for God.

The Lord was with King Jehoshaphat because he walked and sought after Him (2 Chronicles 17:3-4). And because of this, the Lord established the kingdom in his hand and he prospered greatly as all Judah brought him presents. King Jehoshaphat became very rich and honorable. **Riches and honor and length of days do not come by seeking them. They all come by seeking the Lord** (Matthew 6:33). Because of how this man went after the things of God, God caused him to increase in riches. There is no indication that he went looking for these riches. They all came by just seeking the Lord. One of the reasons we do without certain things is because we seek the things and not God, and thereby hinder them from coming to us. The best way to seek riches and honor is by seeking the Lord. When we seek the One who has all riches and honor, we get the riches and honor. This is a great lesson from Jehoshaphat that we also learn from King Solomon (1 Kings 3:1-14).

The richest man that ever lived never sought riches, but sought God and got the riches as a fruit of his relationship with Him. This is still true today and should be the same principle that we apply to our daily lives.

In addition to the riches and honor that King Jehoshaphat received for seeking the Lord, God granted him peace all around Judah. No one made war with Jehoshaphat. Seeking the Lord will cause the fear of God to fall upon all our enemies (Proverbs 16:7). Look at the greatness Jehoshaphat received by just seeking the Lord. Things are sometimes not as hard as we make them. Seeking the Lord is more to our benefit. *"(For after all these things do the Gentiles seek:) for your heavenly Father knoweth that ye have need of all these things. But seek ye first the kingdom of God, and his righteousness; and all these things shall be added unto you"* (Matthew 6:32-33). The Lord has promised to bless the work of our hands (Deuteronomy 24:19). Let us seek the Lord, for this is an easier—and the best—route.

Things were going well for King Jehoshaphat, but then he decided to make friends, alliance and affinity with the wicked (2 Chronicles 18:1). This verse starts by saying *"Now King Jehoshaphat **had riches and honour in abundance**, and joined affinity with Ahab"* (Emphasis mine). Ahab was one of the chief ungodly and wicked kings. Why would a godly man like Jehoshaphat make friends with this evil king Ahab by giving away his child in marriage (affinity)? What good could come from marrying a child of such an evil king? What was he after? He had peace all around him and he had honour in abundance. It's also quite clear that he was doing so well—he was prosperous. He had all the money and then thought he could do whatever he wanted. In his eyes, he had arrived. This is one of the most dangerous positions to be—when everything is going well. The greatest temptation of a man is not when things are terrible, but when all things are going well—when you have success, money, power, and so forth. These times really reveal a lot about a man. Because of pride, we quit seeking and depending on the Lord: after all, we have all these riches and honour. *"And Jehu the son of Hanani the seer went out to meet him, and said to king Jehoshaphat, Shouldest thou help the ungodly, and love them that hate the LORD? there-*

fore is wrath upon thee from before the LORD" (2 Chronicles 19:2).

We should not join in alliance with the ungodly. It causes us to be in position to compromise in an effort to preserve such a relationship. We should not be unequally yoked with unbelievers (2 Corinthians 6:14). This is not only applicable in marriage, but in business and many other affairs. This kind of compromise will most certainly result in sin against the Lord. Jehoshaphat is a good example of this.

Your associations are one of the most important choices you will ever make. Birds of the same feather flock together. We should not be deceived: evil associations negatively affect us (1 Corinthians 15:33). I know some of you might say, "I can be in such a relationship and not be affected. I'm so strong." That's a lie. Sooner or later, you will be affected. It's just a matter of time.

The only exception to this that I can think of is that unless you are in a position of greater influence and ministry to such individuals, you have no business being there. "Blessed is the man that walketh not in the counsel of the ungodly, nor standeth in the way of sinners, nor sitteth in the seat of the scornful. But his delight is in the law of the LORD; and in his law doth he meditate day and night" (Psalms 1:1-2). You should not be driven by such ungodly association. It is very detrimental to your relationship with God. Compromise will become your best friend in such situations.

This relationship with King Ahab eventually put King Jehoshaphat in a compromising situation. He is asked to go to war with Ahab and he accepts, but also asks for a prophet so he can inquire of the Lord on his behalf. When a true prophet (Micaiah) of God was sent, he was being pressured by the messenger of Ahab to "speak good," just as the other four hundred prophets had done. Again, all this happened because of the compromise and affinity that King Jehoshaphat had gotten into with Ahab.

We should never tell a man of God what we want to hear. We should ask and they should speak of their own volition with no pressure and influence. As ministers, we should say what the Lord says, and not what others want to hear (2 Chronicles 18:13). We should have the courage to say what God says and fear not what man has to think. "Let God be true and every man a liar" (Romans 3:4, Proverbs 29:25).

We should avoid blindly doing anything on which we have certain reservations from the Lord (2 Chronicles 18:4, 6). Jehoshaphat should not have been with King Ahab. He knew well this was wrong, but went forward anyway.

Here we see a big mistake for not following the conviction of the Holy Spirit. We should never go against our conscience (Romans 2:15). We should never ever force ourselves to do anything that we know so well is wrong. Saul made the same mistake. He went against what he knew was right in his heart to do what was convenient. His heart was not in agreement. **Every time we sin, we have to violate or go against the voice of God and the witness of God on the inside of us.**

Prepare Our Hearts To Seek The Lord

Our hearts do not just get to know and seek the Lord by themselves. This does not happen naturally without any effort on our part. We must take the initiative and put in the effort to seek the Lord. One of the main things I love about King Jehoshaphat is that he was a man who prepared his heart to seek the Lord (2 Chronicles 19:3). It takes a lot of effort and dedication to seek the Lord. Looking at the leadership of King Rehoboam, we see the very opposite of Jehoshaphat. Rehoboam did not prepare his heart to seek the Lord, and therefore he did evil (2 Chronicles 12:14). **One of the main reasons that we sin and do evil is because we have not prepared our hearts to seek the Lord.** We must make decisions betimes, when there is no pressure and not wait for the time of tragedy to mess up. We must determine what we will do before the opportunity (tragedy, hardship, temptation) comes for us to decide.

We should not only seek the Lord in tragedy, but all the time. It ought to be a lifestyle. If we don't, we may not always get the results we desire. We can't just use God as a microwave or a slot machine where you put in a coin and "God" comes out. If you want to only visit faith in times of trouble, you will not get the same results as those who live by faith (Habakkuk 2:4).

We should seek the Lord every time, and when trouble comes, we will have our fellowship and relationship with the Lord will pull us through. Our endurance, faith, and wisdom will be produced from our continual seeking of the

Lord. Minutes of seeking the Lord will not produce the same results as years of seeking the Lord.

Have you heard someone say, "I prayed just as they did, but I didn't get the same results. Why is it? Is God fair?" Such folks only see the minute-long prayer, but they don't see the years of seeking, fellowship, and preparing our hearts to seek the Lord. It takes time and years to know and grow in the Lord. It is a growth process for each one of us and you should not skip yours because it takes time. We all have to go through a growth process. *"For precept must be upon precept, precept upon precept; line upon line, line upon line; here a little, and there a little: But the word of the LORD was unto them precept upon precept, precept upon precept; line upon line, line upon line; here a little, and there a little;"* (Isaiah 28:10, 13). What we envy, wish for, admire, see, or even desire in other people's lives takes years and years of cultivation, preparation, seeking and fellowshipping with the Lord.

It took someone forty years to get to a place where they do what they do effectively. It did not take just one day of fasting and prayer. There are no shortcuts. You must put in the time. Preparation time is not wasted time.

Although King Jehoshaphat prepared his heart to seek the Lord, He did not do it perfectly. Not all the people sought the Lord like he did. *"And he walked in the way of Asa his father, and departed not from it, doing that which was right in the sight of the LORD. Howbeit the high places were not taken away: for as yet the people had not prepared their hearts unto the God of their fathers"* (2 Chronicles 20:32-

33). Jehoshaphat did not remove the high places, which never should have been erected. Worship was forbidden in any other place but in the temple in Jerusalem.

Rehearse What God Has Done In The Past

It came to pass after this also, that the children of Moab, and the children of Ammon, and with them other beside the Ammonites, came against Jehoshaphat to battle. Then there came some that told Jehoshaphat, saying, There cometh a great multitude against thee from beyond the sea on this side Syria; and, behold, they be in Hazazon-tamar, which is En-gedi. And Jehoshaphat feared, and set himself to seek the LORD, and proclaimed a fast throughout all Judah.

—2 Chronicles 20:1-3

And said, O LORD God of our fathers, art not thou God in heaven? and rulest not thou over all the kingdoms of the heathen? and in thine hand is there not power and might, so that none is able to withstand thee? Art not thou our God, who didst drive out the inhabitants of this land before thy people Israel, and gavest it to the seed of Abraham thy friend forever? And they dwelt therein, and have built thee a sanctuary therein for thy name, saying, If, when evil cometh upon us, as the sword, judgment, or pestilence, or famine, we stand before this house, and in thy presence, (for thy name is in this house,) and cry unto thee in our affliction, then thou wilt hear and help. And now, behold, the children of Ammon and Moab and mount Seir, whom thou wouldest not let Israel invade, when they came out of the land of Egypt, but they turned from them, and destroyed them not; Behold, I say, how they reward us, to come to cast us out of thy possession, which thou hast given us to inherit. O our God, wilt thou not judge them? for we have no might against this great company that cometh against us; neither know we what to do: but our eyes are upon thee. And all Judah stood before the LORD, with their little ones, their wives, and their children. Then upon Jahaziel the son of Zechariah, the son of Benaiah, the son of Jeiel, the son of Mattaniah, a Levite of the sons of Asaph, came the Spirit of the LORD in the midst of the congregation;

—2 Chronicles 20:6-14

Jehoshaphat was being attacked by the Moabites and the Ammonites (2 Chronicles 20). During a difficult time, King Jehoshaphat did not complain but sought the Lord, asked for His help, gave praise, and started rehearsing the victories that God had done in the past (2 Chronicles 20:4-9). This is the right approach in such a time as this. It is also operating in faith. We have to look back at our victories to get hope for today and tomorrow. When we look back, we gain courage to go forward.

Just like Jehoshaphat, we aren't looking or asking for something God has never done before. For everything we face, God has wrought a miracle pertaining to the same in another person's life. Find it and take courage. For example, if you are barren and you want to have children, I know a woman who believed God for about fifteen years, never giving up. Doctors said it was over, her uterus was even removed, but ONE day she conceived and God gave her TRIPLETS! You can receive the same if you believe (Mark 9:28).

Not Against You, Against the Lord

The Moabites and Ammonites were not coming against King Jehoshaphat. It's very clear that those who come against us come against the Lord (2 Chronicles 20:11). Therefore, we should not fear. Fear and dismay are not the same. When one is in fear, they are still functional and not paralyzed. However, dismay is a step beyond fear. The individual is paralyzed by their fear. Because these enemies of Jehoshaphat came against the Lord, the Lord was the One to fight them. This is a very important principle. If someone is coming against you physically, you must fight (John 18:36), but if they are coming against the Lord, or the Lord in you, you must let the Lord fight.

The battle is not ours, but the Lord's (2 Chronicles 20:15). We should therefore cast our cares upon Him (1 Peter 5:7). This is not to say that we sit around waiting for an intervention from God while doing nothing. We must take steps to resolve the problem while believing God to intervene. When the Lord was with Jehoshaphat, it didn't matter who was against him. *What shall we then say to these things? If God be for us, who can be against us?* (Romans 8:31).

Takeaways From Jehoshaphat's Life

One - Words: If they are God's words, and if they are mixed with faith, they are more powerful than swords, bullets, and bombs (Hebrews 4:2).

Two - From Jehoshaphat's life, we learn that true faith will always produce praise. No praise means an absence of true faith and the way we abound in faith is through thanksgiving (Colossians 2:7). He praised God before AND after his victory. Many people can praise Jesus after, but few can do it before. We should praise the Lord before and after the victory. **True men of faith will always praise God at both sides of the Red Sea** (Exodus 15:1).

Three - The Lord is never late. He is seldom early. The enemies of Jehoshaphat were not destroyed the day before when they started to believe God. He didn't even do it three to four days before when they began to seek the Lord. He was right on time. He was neither late nor early. We can count on God to come through for us, even if it looks like the last minute. Even if it looks like it's late, let us believe His messengers or prophets. When we do, we get godly vision (2 Chronicles 20:20)!

Four - The Lord has a variety of ways to meet the needs of his people or to bring them victory. The Lord employed different strategies almost every time He took on his enemies. We should not put Him in a box and think He can only do it this way and not another way. Here, He pulled a unique strategy on His enemies. They were stunned (2 Chronicles 20:23-24). Notice the result of believing and trusting in the

Lord. The very problem that was meant to kill and destroy them turned out to be the greatest blessing (Romans 8:28). They gathered spoils for three days. This was huge! Hallelujah! They were greatly increased by those who sought to kill and destroy them (2 Chronicles 20:25).

Conclusion

Life is a life full of lessons. We learn from those who went before us and those who are with us. There are different forms of learning: positively or negatively. We learn what to do and apply in our lives or we can learn what NOT to do. We can learn through the Word or through the school of hard knocks.

One thing I do not recommend is always learning by experience. Sometimes the best way is to learn from the experience of another. Then, you will have no scars, but you have still learned a thing or two. You do not have to go through some tragedy to learn how bad and detrimental it can be to you. You can learn at another man's expense (1 Corinthians 10:1-12). If people only learn by experience then our learning is going to be limited because it is practically impossible to learn everything by personal experience.

In this book, I have laid out a few things about the kings I have personally studied. I have found this very helpful and I started to apply it to my life. There is so much to learn, but we can take it step by step and apply these great virtues in our lives while watching for the traps they fell into.

My prayer is that you will learn a lot from these kings and then apply it to your life as you also share what you have learned with another. My heart is to change lives, one at a time, helping them mature in their walk with God and become disciples of the Lord by pointing people to Jesus and His Word. Thank you for taking time to read this book. I hope it has touched your life in a very unique way.

Receive Jesus As Your Savior

Deciding to receive Jesus Christ as your Lord and Savior is the most important decision you'll ever make! Nothing comes close to this decision; not your career and not even your spouse. It will change your life now and your eternal destiny. There is no decision that could be made that is like it. It would be very sad for me to teach you that Jesus was and is God and not give you an opportunity to repent and to receive Him into your heart as your God and Savior. Will you accept Him as God and not just another good man like some believe and say?

God has promised, *"If thou shalt confess with thy mouth the Lord Jesus, and shalt believe in thine heart that God hath raised him from the dead, thou shalt be saved. For with the heart man believeth unto righteousness; and with the mouth confession is made unto salvation.... For whosoever shall call upon the name of the Lord shall be saved"* (Romans 10:9-10, 13).

By His grace, God has already done everything on His part to provide for your salvation. Your part is simply to believe and receive. It is the easiest decision. This is a heart decision, not a head decision. Now is the acceptable time, today is the day of salvation (2 Corinthians 6:2). Why wait?

Pray this prayer and mean it sincerely from your heart:

Jesus,
I confess that You are my Lord and Savior. I believe in my heart that God raised You from the dead. By

faith in Your Word, I receive salvation, now. Thank You for saving me!

The very moment you commit your life to Jesus Christ, the truth of His Word instantly comes to pass in your spirit. Now that you are born again, you are brand new on the inside. God has created in you a new spirit and a new heart.

Receive the Baptism of the Holy Spirit

Living a Christian life is not just a difficult thing to do, but an impossible thing. You need help. So, because it is impossible to live a victorious, Christian life without the baptism of the Holy Spirit, the Lord wants to give you the supernatural power you need to live this new life. We receive power when we receive the baptism of the Holy Spirit (Acts 1:8).

It's as simple as asking and receiving. When we ask for the Holy Spirit, the Lord will give Him to us (Luke 11:10, 13).

All you have to do is ask, believe, and receive! Pray:

Father,

I recognize my need for Your power to live this new life. Please fill me with Your Holy Spirit. By faith, I receive Him right now! Thank You for baptizing me. Holy Spirit, You are welcome in my life.

Congratulations! Now you are filled with God's supernatural power. Some syllables from a language you don't recognize will rise up from your heart to your mouth (See 1 Corinthians 14:14). Go ahead and speak those syllables. As you speak them out loud by faith, you're releasing God's power from within and building yourself up in the Spirit (See 1 Corinthians 14:4). You can do this whenever and wherever you like.

It does not really matter whether you felt anything or not when you prayed to receive the Lord and His Spirit. If you believed in your heart that you received, then God's Word promises that you received. "*Therefore I say unto you, What things soever ye desire, when ye pray, believe that ye receive them, and ye shall have them*" (Mark 11:24). God always honors His Word—believe it!

About The Author

Rich was born and raised in Kampala, Uganda, where he lived until after high school when he received Christ into his heart. After he became a born-again Christian, God opened a door for him to go to India and pursue a Bachelor of Commerce at Garden City College (University) in Bangalore graduating in 2010. While in India, he was ordained a teacher and leader at his local church tasked with leading and teaching the adult Sunday School. He also established his first Bible study group with a few students at Garden City College. Since then, he has been establishing groups and teaching God's Word.

He later moved to the United States where God spoke to him to go to Charis Bible College and prepare for the ministry that God had called him. He graduated in 2017 with a Masters in Biblical Studies and a license to preach the gospel of Jesus Christ. He has been teaching and bringing godly insight to the scriptures since 2008.

He is a seasoned student of the Word and a teacher by gifting and calling. Rich's passion is to teach God's Word to the body of Christ with a greater emphasis on grace, faith, and making disciples. He is the author of *Jesus; God or Man?* and *Good Health and Long Life: Another Perspective*. Rich also serves as the Assistant Dean of Education at Charis Bible College in Woodland Park, CO.

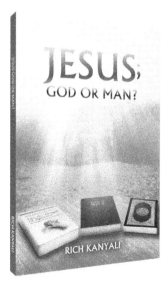

Jesus; God or Man?

by Rich Kanyali

Paperback

ISBN: 978-1513627113

In this book, Mr. Kanyali takes you on a journey to discover a certain truth that distinguishes Christianity from any other religion, faith or belief system. Have you ever given a single thought as to whether Jesus was God or man?

To some, Jesus was a good man. To some, He was a great historical figure. To some, He was god (not divine). To some, He was a god among many other gods. To some, an angel (Michael the archangel). To some, a prophet, but to others, He was and is God. So, which is which? What category do you fall into? Was Jesus God or man? Within the pages of this book, you will find powerful biblical proof and sound reasoning to who Jesus truly was and is. The evidence is within the pages of this book. The truth is unveiled leaving no stone unturned. Reading this book will shed light on your understanding and give you a greater revelation of this truth.

Available on:
- Richkanyaliministries.com
- Amazon
- Barnes and Noble
- Books a Million
- eBook also available

Good Health and Long life: Another Perspective

by Rich Kanyali

Paperback

ISBN: 978-1642044201

Good Health & Long Life—Another Perspective is written to give a different perspective on Health and Long life. Many times, the only focus on health is what we do physically such as what we eat, how we exercise and so forth. However, there is a very much untapped side of health which is even more important than the physical. In this book, I explore this side and how we can enhance our health and achieve long life.

Available on:
- Richkanyaliministries.com
- Amazon
- Barnes and Noble
- Books a Million